T0117011

Come on Down to My Place and Get Something to Eat!
A Tailgating Party Cookbook

iUniverse books may be ordered through booksellers or by contacting:

iUniverse
1663 Liberty Drive
Bloomington, IN 47403
www.iuniverse.com
1 800-Authors (1-800-288-4677)

ISBN: 978-1-4620-3707-0 (sc)
ISBN: 978-1-4620-3708-7 (e)

Printed in the United States of America

iUniverse rev. date: 9/19/2011

COME ON DOWN TO MY PLACE AND GET SOMETHING TO EAT!

A TAILGATING PARTY COOKBOOK

CELEBRATING AN AMERICAN HERITAGE:
TAILGATING AT HISTORICALLY BLACK COLLEGES
AND UNIVERSITIES (HBCUs) HOMECOMINGS AND
FOOTBALL GAMES BEFORE, AFTER THE GAME, IN
THE PARKING LOTS AND ON THE CAMPUSES

RECIPES FOR APPETIZERS, ENTREES, DESSERTS
AND HOMECOMING SPIRITS

MADE IN BATCHES AND IN STYLE

BY

SHARON HUNT, MS, RD, LD

Go Wildcats!   Go Rattlers!
Go Tigers!   Go Pirates!
Go Panthers!   Go Bison!
Go Dragons!   Go Bears!
Go Lions!   Go Spartans!
Go Hornets!   Go Aggies!

iUniverse, Inc.
Bloomington

Table of Contents

FOREWORD

This cookbook is dedicated to all tailgaters at Historically Black Colleges and Universities (HBCUs) football games. The perseverance, love, money, food and hospitality offered to fellow classmates, family and friends can be enormous. It is all FUN!

Recipes are given for appetizers, entrees, desserts and homecoming spirits. These are my versions of recipes to serve fifty people.

Only Historically Black Colleges and Universities (HBCUs) with football programs will be highlighted throughout the recipe section.

To My Many Friends: You Do The Math: Make As Many Corrections, Deletions Or Additions As You Deem Necessary! Add As Many Notes As You Can!

Mathew 4.4
It is written, man shall not live by bread alone, but by every word that proceedth out of the mouth of God.

PREFACE

This book is designed for tailgaters who have fun preparing southern food and feeding large groups. These recipes are just for fun. They do not represent a certain group of HBCUs. The recipes are the author's choices from known tailgaters. Most products are from Georgia.

In this Tailgating Party Cookbook, a bit of history of each college and university with a football program in the five divisions are highlighted. Interesting facts about the nicknames of the football team and the college bands at each school are included with a brief history.

Each HBCUs has a traditional method of celebrating homecoming. Another purpose for writing the cookbook is to bring attention to the growing popularity of homecoming and tailgating activities around campuses.

ACKNOWLEDGEMENTS

I wish to thank all of the people who assisted me in the development of this book. A special "Thank You!" goes out to my many ancestors who fought hard for developing and maintaining the need for Historically Black Colleges and Universities (HBCUs).

I express my congratulations to all football coaches and teams. A special 'shout out' to the all the coaches and football players since 1975 at Fort Valley State University.

Most of all I want to thank those people who gave me some of the menus and recipes for tailgating.

I give my heart to all my Hunt brothers who played and excelled at football at Wewoka High School in Wewoka, Oklahoma

-Dewey, Jr, Elgin Wayne, Jerry Allen, Dahlton, Paul Dexter, Ray Dean, Randy, Dandy, Barry Keith and Llewellyn.

ABOUT THE AUTHOR

Sharon K. Hunt is an associate professor in food and nutrition. She has more than twenty years in research and teaching food and nutrition. She has taught at two Historically Black Universities.

Ms. Sharon Kaye Hunt, RD, LD, is a retired Associate Professor in the Department of Family and Consumer Sciences at Fort Valley State University. She is an author of four books, six cookbooks, twelve children books and one historical book. Ms. Hunt appeared three times on QVC Home Shopping Network selling her cookbook –Bread from Heaven. Her historical book – 83 Imprisoned in the Garden of Evil - centers around the U.S. Colored Troops who were prisoners of war at Andersonville, Georgia during the Civil War.

For many years, Ms. Hunt worked with the FVSU Queens coronation committee. She wrote a booklet to assist the queens in preparing for the coronation. Ms. Hunt is also the author of the original recipe for the 'World Largest Peach Cobbler' showcased at the Fort Valley Peach Festival, Fort Valley, Georgia each year in June. Also, Ms. Hunt has served as an Artist–in-Residence at the Georgia National Fair in Perry, Georgia. A member of Delta Sigma Theta Sorority, Inc., Ms. Hunt served as charter president of the Warner Robins Alumnae Chapter.

INTRODUCTION

OBJECTIVES FOR WRITING THE TAILGATING
COOKBOOK

The objectives of the cookbook are to:

◘ Provide a tailgating cookbook for recipes made for 50 people or more;
◘ Introduce the method of cooking handed down African-Americans recipes;
◘ Provide historical information for the coming generations;
◘ Establish significance and beneficial of quantity recipes and contribution cooking procedures, and
◘ Generate interest in homecoming at Historically Black Colleges and Universities

Psalm 71.1
In thee, O Lord, do I put my trust; let me never be put in confusion

ORGANIZATION FOR
THE COOKBOOK

The HBCUs cookbook has been organized so that one can evaluate the historical overview of the HBCUs and the major conferences showing this school. The history of each conference is given with football programs of the HBCUs in each conference. Tidbits on schools' history have been given. The tailgaters menus are listed next: appetizers, entrée, dessert and Homecoming Spirits. The beverages listed are wines. The wine recipes are written in a common fashion. They are just for fun. These menus and recipes do not represent any school in particular.

TAILGATING PARTY COOKBOOK - MENUS AND RECIPES

There are suggested menus recipes for appetizers, entrees, desserts and Homecoming Spirits. Each recipe serves a minimum of fifty servings. However, some recipes may serve more than the bottom line of fifty. The first item on the menu is the appetizer. The appetizer is a popular item used to accompany the entrée or a popular item used in tailgating. This product may be a snack, salad, grilled fruits, grilled vegetables or other dish. Some of these foods maybe prepared hours before the big day or purchased as a convenience food.

The entrée is the main meat dish. Georgians during tailgating season not only grill or barbecue red meats, white meats or vegetables for the main dish but they also deep-fat fry, stew or boil items for the main dish. On a cold day at a football game, the Georgia tailgaters may prepare hot chili, Brunswick stew, Gumbo, Jambalaya or Hot Tilapia or fried whiting fish.

The desserts may be prepared ahead and served from the grill, served from a cooler or prepared on the grill. The idea is to show nutritious desserts as well as cutting calories.

The beverage, which is always a homemade wine, is noted in the plural form — Homecoming spirits. This is sort of a nickname in celebration of the activity and for the gathering of friends. These homemade wines are carryovers from the sharecropper or plantation past long ago. It was a common heritage that people would make all kinds of wines during the summer from leftover fruits or vegetables including wild grapes or fruits that would taste good. Tailgaters always get together so that there is no duplication of menu items.

I have written this book from notes of a collection of tailgaters I have visited from over the years. For the recipes to serve fifty adults, I have extended each recipe. There are many tailgaters and their menus. Each tailgater is a resident of Georgia and they either list their many professions or their handle (a football name).

Slavery and HBCUs

Slaves — First slaves came to Jamestown, Virginia in 1619.

Number of first Slaves — Approximately Twenty Million slaves captured during slavery.

Slavery Period — 1619 to 1865 Middle Passage

Emancipation Proclamation — freed slaves. Prior to emancipation for more than 200 years, the slaves were considered three-fifths of a human being.

HBCUs for African Americans — First records of Historically Black College and Universities in the United States were Cheyney University 1837 and Lincoln University in Lincoln, Pennsylvania in 1854.

What are HBCUs?

Historically Black Colleges and Universities

After the Civil War, the Freedman Bureau was established to assist freed slaves in many ways. One of the establishments was higher education.

Historically Black Colleges and Universities are located in many states. Cheyney University of Pennsylvania is the oldest.

Lincoln University is the second HBCUs in the United States. The third school was Wilberforce University founded in 1855.

Freedman's Bureau Office, Northern Churches and religious societies instituted colleges, universities across the South in the 1860's and the 1870's. Examples include: Fisk in Tennessee, Hampton in Virginia, Tougalou in Mississippi and several schools in South Carolina.

The American Baptist Home Mission Society founded Virginia's Union, Shaw in North Carolina, and Benedict in South Carolina and Morehouse in Georgia. North Methodist assisted in establishing Claflin in South Carolina, Rust in Mississippi and Bennett in North Carolina.

The Episcopalians were responsible for the St. Augustine in North Carolina and St. Paul in Virginia.

Mathew 4.19:
Follow me and I will make you fishers of men.

WHAT ARE HBCUs?

Historically Black Colleges and Universities?

After the Civil War, the Freedman Bureau was established to assist freed slaves in many ways. One of the establishments was schools, especially in higher education.

Historically Black Colleges and Universities are located in many southern states. However, oldest HBCU5 are Cheyney University in Pennsylvania in 1837 and Lincoln University in Lincoln Pennsylvania in 1854.

Freedman Bureau

Congress established the Freedman's Bureau in March 1865. The purpose of the Bureau was to provide transition from slavery to freedom. The Bureau assisted ex-slaves with food, clothing and transportation and the Bureau monitored labor contracts and settled freedman and abandoned or confiscated land. Also, among the Freedmen Bureau responsibilities were to maintain schools for black children. Oliver Otis Howard, the Freedman Bureau Commissioner, was a founder of Howard University.

Since the Civil War, African Americans have been seeking interest at HBCU. These schools have distinguished themselves not only in academics, but also in sports. Sports have improved the schools images, brought attention to the academic programs.

The purpose of this Cookbook is to bring attention to the growing popularity of tailgating or parties around the campus.

○ ○ ○

HBCUs

"YOU ARE THE CHOSEN GENERATION A ROYAL PRIESTHOOD, A HOLY NATION." His own special people, that you may proclaim the praises of Him who called you out of darkness into His marvelous light. (1 Peter 2:9).

CLASSIFICATIONS

2000 Carnegie Classifications of HBCUs

Doctoral/Research Universities — Extensive (Dr. Ext)

Howard University	DC

Doctoral/Research Universities — Intensive (Dr. Int)

Alabama A&M University	AL
Clark Atlanta University	GA
Jackson State University	MS
South Carolina State University	SC
Tennessee State University	TN
Texas Southern University	TX
Virginia University	VA

Masters (Comprehensive) Colleges and Universities I — (MAI)

Alabama State University	AL
Tuskegee University	AL
Delaware State University	DE
University of District of Columbia	DC
Florida A&M University	FL
Albany State University	GA
Fort Valley State University	GA
Chicago State University	IL

Grambling State University	LA
Southern University, A&M at BR	LA
Xavier University	LA
Bowie State University	MD
Coppin State University	MD
University of MD E Shore	MD
Lincoln University	MD
Alcorn State University	MS
Fayette State University	NC
North Carolina A&T University	NC
North Carolina Central University	NC
Cheyney University	PA
Lincoln University	PA
Prairie View at University of Texas	TX
Hampton University	VA
Norfolk State University	VA
Virginia State University	VA

Master's (Comprehensive) Colleges and Universities II — (MAII)

Savannah State University	GA
Kentucky State University	KY
Southern University at New Orleans	LA
University of the Virgin Islands	VI

Baccalaureate Colleges/Liberal Arts (BALA)

Fayetteville State Universit	NC
North Carolina A&T University	NC
North Carolina Central University	NC
Cheyney University	PA
Lincoln University	PA
Prairie View at University of Texas	TX

Hampton University	VA
Norfolk State University	VA
Virginia State University	VA

Master's (Comprehensive) Colleges and Universities II-(MAII)

Savannah State University	GA
Kentucky State University	KY
Southern University at New Orleans	LA
University of the Virgin Islands	VI

Baccalaureate Colleges/Liberal Arts (BALA)

Talladega College	AL
Arkansas Baptist College	AR
Morehouse College	GA
Paine College	GA
Spelman College	GA
Tougaloo College	MS
Bennett College	NC
St. Augustine College	FL
Fisk University	TN
Lane College	TN
Texas College	TX

Baccalaureate College/General (BAGEN)

Miles College	AL
Oakwood College	AL
Stillman College	AL
University of Arkansas at PB	AR
University of Arkansas at PB	AR
Bethune Cookman College	FL
Edward Waters College	FL

Florida Memorial College	FL
Morris Brown College	GA
Dillard University	LA
Mississippi Valley State University	MS
Rust College	MS
Medgar Evers College	NY
Elizabeth City State University	NC
Johnson C. Smith University	NC
Livingstone College	NC
Shaw University	NC
Winston-Salem State University	NC
Central State University	OH
Wilberforce University	OH
Langston University	SC
Allen University	SC
Benedict College	SC
Claflin College	SC
Morris College	SC
Voorhees College	SC
LeMoyne-Owen College	TN
Huston-Tillotson College	TX
Jarvis Christian College	TX
Paul Quinn College	TX
St. Paul's College	VA
Bluefield State College	WV
West Virginia State College	WV
Concordia College	AL

Associate's Colleges

Bishop State College	AL

J.F. Drake State Tech	AL
Lawson State Community College	AL
Compton Community College	CA
Southern University Shreveport	LA
Lewis College of Business	MI
Coahoma Junior College	MS
Hinds Community College	MS
Mary Holmes College	MS
St. Philips College	TX

Theological Seminars Related Institutions (Faith)

Interdenominational Theological Center	GA
Southwestern Christian	TX

Schools of Business and Management (BUS)

Wiley College	TX

Medical Schools and Medical Centers (MED)

Morehouse School of Medicine	GA
Meharry Medical College	TN

Teachers Colleges (TEACH)

Harris Stowe	MD

Source,
Carnegie Foundation
2000

Second Morrill Act
1890 Land Grant Colleges and Universities

(August 3, 1890 —The second Morrill Act was passed providing for separate land grant institutions for persons of color.)

Institution

Lincoln University	1866
Alcorn State University	1871
South Carolina State College	1872
University of Arkansas at Pine Bluff	1873
Alabama A&M University	1875
Prairie View A&M University	1876
Southern University	1880
Tuskegee University	1881
Virginia State University	1882
Kentucky State University	1886
Florida A&M University	1887
Delaware State University	1881
North Carolina A&T University	1881
Fort Valley State University	1895
Langston University	1897
Tennessee State University	1912

Definition of Land Grant: Colleges who through the Morrill Act of 1890 were officially established.

SHORT HISTORY OF FRATERNITIES AND SORORITIES

1. Alpha Phi Alpha Fraternity December 6, 1906 Cornel University
2. Alpha Kappa Alpha Sorority January 15, 1908 Howard University
3. Kappa Alpha Psi Fraternity January 12, 1911
4. Omega Psi Phi Fraternity November 17, 1911 Howard University
5. Delta Sigma Theta Sorority January 13, 1913 was Founded by 22 collegiate women at Howard University.
6. Phi Beta Sigma fraternity January 9, 1914 was founded by three young men at Howard University
7. Zeta Phi Beta Sorority January 16, 1920 Howard University
8. Sigma Gamma Rho Sorority November 12 1922

List of Historically Black Colleges and Universities and their Established Date

University	Location	Year Founded
Alabama		
Alabama A&M University	Huntsville	1875
Alabama State University	Montgomery	1867
Bishop State Community College	Mobile	1927
Concordia College	Selma	1922
Gadsden State Community College	Gadsden	2003
JF Drake State Technical College	Huntsville	1961
Lawson State Community College	Birmingham	1973
Miles College	Fairfield	1905
Oakwood College	Huntsville	1843
Selma University	Selma	1878
Shelton State Community College	Tuscaloosa	1979
Stillman College	Tuscaloosa	1876
Talladega College	Talladega	1867
Trenholm State Technical College	Montgomery	2001
Tuskegee Institute/University	Tuskegee	1881
Arkansas		
Arkansas Baptist College	Little Rock	1884
Philander Smith College	Little Rock	1887
University of Arkansas at Pine Bluff	Pine Bluff	1873

| Delaware State University | Dover | 1891 |

Washington, DC
| Howard University | Washington, DC | 1867 |
| U. of the District of Columbia | Washington, DC | 1976 |

Florida
Bethune Cookman College	Daytona Beach	1904
Edward Waters College	Jacksonville	1866
Florida A&M University	Tallahassee	1887
Florida Memorial College	Miami	1879

Georgia
Albany State University	Albany	1903
Clark Atlanta University	Atlanta	1988
Fort Valley State University	Fort Valley	1895
Interdenominational Theological Ctr	Atlanta	1958
Morehouse College	Atlanta	1867
Morehouse School of Medicine	Atlanta	1975
Morris Brown College	Atlanta	1881
Paine College	Augusta	1882
Savannah State College	Savannah	1890
Spelman College	Atlanta	1881

Kentucky
| Kentucky State University | Frankfort | 1886 |

Louisiana
| Dillard University | New Orleans | 1930 |
| Grambling State University | Grambling | 1901 |

Southern University A&M College	Baton Rouge	1880
Southern University at New Orleans	New Orleans	1956
Southern University of Shreveport	Shreveport	1967
Xavier University	New Orleans	1925

Maryland

Bowie State University	Bowie	1865
Coppin State College	Baltimore	1900
Morgan State University	Baltimore	1867
University of Maryland Eastern Shore	Princess Ann	1948

Michigan

Lewis College of Business	Detroit	1928

Alcom State University	Alcorn	1871
Caohoma Community College	Clarksdale	1949
Jackson State University	Jackson	1877
Mary Holmes College	West Point	1892
Mississippi Valley State University	Itta Bena	1950
Rust College	Holly Springs	1866
Tougaloo College	Tougaloo	1869

Missouri

Harris-Stowe State College	St. Louis	1857
Lincoln University	Jefferson City	1866

North Carolina

Barber-Scotia College	Concord	1867

Bennett College	Greensboro	1873
Elizabeth City State University	Elizabeth City	1891
Fayetteville State University	Fayetteville	1867
Johnson C. Smith University	Charlotte	1867
Livingstone College	Salisbury	1879
North Carolina A&T University	Greensboro	1891
North Carolina Central University	Durham	1910
Shaw University	Raleigh	1865
St. Augustine' College	Raleigh	1867
Winston-Salem State University	Winston-Salem	1892

Ohio

Central State University	Wilberforce	1887
Wilberforce University	Wilberforce	1856

Oklahoma

Langston University	Langston	1897

Pennsylvania

Cheney University of Pennsylvania	Cheney	1837
Lincoln University	Lincoln	1854

South Carolina

Allen University	Columbia	1870
Benedict College	Columbia	1870
Claflin College/University	Orangeburg	1869
Clinton Junior College	Rock Hill	1894
Denmark Technical College	Denmark	1947
Morris College	Sumter	1908

| South Carolina State University | Orangeburg | 1896 |
| Voorhees College | Den more | 1897 |

Tennessee

Fisk University	Nashville	1866
Knoxville College	Knoxville	1875
Lane College	Jackson	1882
LeMoyne Owens College	Memphis	1968
McHarry Medical College	Nashville	1876
Tennessee State University	Nashville	1912

Texas

Huston-Tillotson College	Austin	1952
Jarvis Christian College	Hawkins	1912
Paul Quinn College	Dallas	1872
Prairie View A&M University	Prairie View	1876
Southwestern Christian College	Terrell	1948
St. Phillip's College	San Antonio	1898
Texas College	Tyler	1894
Texas Southern University	Houston	1947
Wiley College	Marshall	1873

Virgin Islands

| University of Virgin Island | St. Thomas | 1962 |

Virginia

Hampton University	Hampton	1868
Norfolk State University	Norfolk	1935
St. Paul's College	Petersburg	1865
Virginia State University	Petersburg	1865
Virginia Union University	Richmond	1865

West Virginia

Bluefield State College	Bluefield	1895
West Virginia State College	Institute	1865

SLAVE VIGNETTES

Slave Sales

There were two legal places for sailing slaves in Augusta; Lower Market, at the corner of Fifth and Broad Street, and Upper Market at the corner of Broad and Karbury Streets. The slave quarters are still standing I Hamburg, S.C., directly in the Savannah River from the Lower Market in Augusta. Slaves were to be put for for sale were kept there until the legal of sales.

Advertisements is the newspapers of that day seem to point the fact that most slave sales were the results of the death of the master, and the consequent settlement of estates, or a result of the foreclosure of mortgage.

In the Thirty-Seven Section of the Ordinance of the City Augusta, August 10, 1820— July 8, 1829, is the following Warning Vendue Masters:

"If any person acts as a Vendue Master within the limits of City without license from the City Council, he shall be fined sum not exceeding $1,000.00. There shall not be more than four in Masters for this city. They shall be appointed by ballot, their license shall expire on the day proceeding the 1st Saturday October of every year. No license shall be issued to a Vendue until he has given bond, with securities according to the laws of a State, and also a bond with approved security to the Council the faithful discharge of his duties in the sum of $5,000.00."

The newspapers of the time regularly carried advertisements about the sale of slaves. The following is a fair sample: sell slaves: With this farm will be sold about Thirty Likely Negroes mostly country bon, among them a very good bricklayer, and driver, and two sawyers, 17 of them are fit for field or boat work, and the rest fine, thriving children."

The following advertisement appeared in The Georgia Constitutionalist on January 17, 1769; "To be sold in Savannah on Thursday the 15th inst. A cargo of 140 Prime Slaves, chiefly men, just arrived in the Scow Gambia Captain Nicholas Doyle after a passage of six weeks directly from the River Gambia" by Inglis and Hall.

Most of the advertisements gave descriptions of each slave, with his age and the type of work he could do. They were generally advertised along with other property belonging to the slave owner.

The following appeared in the Chronicle and Sentinel of Augusta on December 23rd, 1864: "Negro Sales. At an auction in Columbus the annexed prices were obtained: a boy 16 years old, $3,625."

"At a late sale in Wilmington the annexed prices were obtained: a girl 14 years old $5,400; a girl 22 years old, $4,850; a girl 13 years $3,500; a negro boy, 22 years old $4,900."

Very few of the slaves interviewed had passed through the bitter experienced of being sold. Janie Satterwhite, who was born on a Carolina Plantation, and was about thirteen years old when she was freed, remembered very distinctly when she was sold away from her parents.

- Georgia Slaves
- WPA Interviews

♦ ♦ ♦

Letter Published in Macon Telegraph

The Telegraph
P.O. Box 4167
Macon, Ga. 3 1208-4167
2008

Dear Sir:

One of the greatest gifts our slave ancestors gave us is the gift of forgiveness. Most of them forgave their slave owners. The slaves practiced the lesson taught by Jesus Christ: forgive them because they did not know what they were doing. With forgiveness, the slaves were able to endure with or without an apology. Down through the years, they were able to produce the likes of Condelezza Rice, Oprah Winfrey, Tiger Woods, Dr. Martin Luther King, Jr. and many, many more leaders and professionals.

State Senator Robert Brown defined slavery correctly, however, all Americans should learn about the contributions slaves gave to early America and especially to Georgia without pay and housing. Since we are about to celebrate the anniversary of the Civil War, all facets should be studied by all cultures. Slaves used to say "in due time, what goes around, comes around".

Sharon Hunt
Warner Robins
923-6439

What is Homecoming?

Homecoming Week

The week begins on the Sunday before the homecoming football game and ends on the Sunday after the game. The administrators, faculty, staff and students, alumni, friends from all over the world are welcomed to all of the events.

The alumni schedule activities as well as the University; some of the activities are jointly scheduled. The alumni schedule will be assigned to the outline of scheduled activities for each day and night of the homecoming week. The homecoming week takes place usually during the month of October or first week in November. Each day has a theme.

ANOTHER PURPOSE OF HISTORICALLY BLACK COLLEGES AND UNIVERSITIES (HBCUs) HOMECOMING

Due to the historical circumstances surrounding the HBCU's, presidents and alumni retain elements of African culture to celebrate the beginning of the schools' early history showing that only segregation was the way of life for former slaves. The schools were run on "leftovers" from other institutions.

Because the schools were left to survive on their own, the schools created songs, dances, music and foodways indigenous to the region and began a new culture. Homecoming celebrations, gospel music, plays, dances, step shows competitions, and celebrations of alumni success.

SAMPLE HOMECOMING PROGRAM

SCHEDULE OF HOMECOMING ACTIVITIES

Sunday
During homecoming celebration an entire week from Sunday through Sunday is celebrated around the University's heritage. Sunday begins with a celebration of gospel music — the traditions from anthems, hymns, scriptures and operatic gospel down through the years from Africa.

HOMECOMING SUNDAY
The occasion is marked with songs from slavery to Thomas Dorsey to the hip-hop generation. Also, you may see some stumpers, steppers, as well as, mimes. The major impact one will see is the gift of song, especially, the Gospel Explosion.

Praise through Song
Anthems -OPENING HYMN — NEGRO SPIRITUALS or Slave Songs

WE ARE CLIMBING JACOB'S LADDER

We are climbing Jacob's ladder
We are climbing Jacob's ladder
We are climbing Jacob's ladder

Soldiers of the Cross
Soldiers of the Cross
Brothers of the Cross
Brothers of the Cross
Sisters of the Cross
Sisters of the Cross

Every round goes higher and higher
Every round goes higher and higher
Every round goes higher and higher
Soldiers of the Cross
Sinner do you love your Jesus?
If you love him, why not serve him?
Rise, Shine, give God the glory
Soldiers of the Cross

SAMPLE OF SONG FEST AT THE GOSPEL EXPLOSION

- Choirs
- Hymns
- Choirs
- Groups

Praise Through Spirits
- Sermons
- Dance
- Stumpers
- Steppers
- Mimes

Speaking in Tongues

The Fisk Jubilee Singers were among the first groups of college singers who toured America and Europe to support their University. They sang slave songs and popular songs. The Fisk Jubilee singers earned enough funds to fund Jubilee Hall. Fisk first formed the building which is now designated as a national Historic Landmark.

Monday — Official Homecoming Kickoff Week

The school's pep rallies and seminars are a formal affair. Usually the president introduces the head coach, assistant coaches, football team and the administration. The band and cheerleaders lead the university in to a homecoming pep rally Monday — Homecoming Week Kickoff.

12:00 — All campus community meet in the gymnasium

- Mock trial of the opposing football team (Skit)
- Introductions of coaches, teams and other team's personnel
- President speaks and gives away prizes

Monday afternoon and evening

- Everyone dresses out — Campus colors

- Campus buildings and fraternities and sorority houses are decorated

Monday Night
- Paint the town
- Student paint windows of stores in the downtown area and streets with the paws of the mascot (Tigers, Wildcats)
- Campus life comes alive
- Homecoming concert in Campus Complex
- * Alumni — make last minute plans

Tuesday — Dress in School Colors
University Students' Day
Noon — Campus novelty, T-Shirt wearing day
- Night activity— Intramural basketball
- Night movie on the lawn
- Midnight breakfast — cafeteria

Wednesday — University Students Day
The main theme of the campus is the homecoming slogan. Each organization and dormitory centers decorate on the theme. Students spend time in class and decorating for the big day. Also, the marching band will be practicing for the big day. A high point of the day will be the celebration of special foods-foods from the part or foods commonly prepared in the area-simple menus: Taste of Louisiana, Taste of the Valley, Taste of Alabama or Taste of the name of the school mascot.

Sample Alumni Activities
Alumni Village
- ◻ Alumni meet and greet old friends and classmates
- ◻ Purchase alumni merchandise (caps, shirts, car tags, sleepers, pens, cuff links, patches, pens, cups, etc.)
- ◻ Catch up on the local news of the University

Homecoming Parade
- ◻ Alumni participate in the parade (arrangements should be made for all activities)
- ◻ Vehicles — Floats
- ◻ Walking/Dancing Unit

Alumni Dance
Alumni have a big dance in a local city auditorium or special place for a fee. Usually an outstanding band is the focal point.

Cook-off
A Bar-B-Q cook-off is a norm draw for the alumni

Class Reunion
- Special year graduates are planned for formal gatherings

The office of Alumni affairs usually coordinates all alumni activities

Tailgating
Alumni apply for special spots almost a year in advance

Golf Tournament

Alumni Tours
- New Building — Grounds award winning activities

Noon — Student Union
- Student comedians all afternoon until 9:00 a.m. p.m.
7:00 p.m. — Step show — non-Greek
9:00 p.m. — Professional comedian
10:00 p.m. — After Party — Student Center or Union

Thursday -FORMER HOMECOMING Queens' Day
- Queens's convocation
- Former queen gives address and other queens in attendance along with interested students
- Morning — Queen's Brunch

Afternoon — Homecoming Queen's Tea

Thursday night — Homecoming Queen's Coronation Program
- Opening Interlude
- Master and Mistress of Ceremony
- Organizational queens introduced prelude to the class queens
- Homecoming queen walks on the red carpet to the front of the stage
- Queen's gives a speech and then she is crowned by the president, captain of the football teams and former queen
- Royal Court - Royal Dance

5:00 p.m. — Wildcat tailgating begins — designated area

Friday- Alumni Day
Alumni Arrival
7:00 a.m. —Alumni arrival
8:00 a.m. — Arrival alumni — Golf Tournament
9:30 a.m. — Alumni Induction in the Hall of Fame
1:00 p.m. — 5:00 p.m. — Block Party/1 Yard fest/Campus
Noon — Scholarship and Awards Luncheon
2:00 p.m. — Luncheon Alumni Meeting
9:00 p.m. — 2:00 a.m. — Alumni Mixer — Local hotel
8:30 p.m. — University Fraternity Sorority Step Show
9:00 p.m. — Old School Jam
11:00 p.m. — Fraternity and sorority paraphernalia party — Student Union

Saturday University Victory Day
9:00 a.m. — Homecoming Parade
　　　Led by Parade Marshall

Homecoming Parade
The homecoming activities will begin while the homecoming parade comes through downtown and throughout the campus. The Parade Marshall rides in a special car and the president along with other dignitaries ride in the front of the parade.

Viewing Stand for Presidential Party

12:00 pm. — Cook-off Barbeque

1:30 p.m. - **GAME TIME - OPEN WITH THE SINGING OF THE** NATIONAL

ANTHEM AND SING THE NEGRO NATIONAL ANTHEM
-NATIONAL ANTHEM
Star Spangled Banner (National Anthem 1931 written in September 1814 by Frances
Scott Key)
Oh, say, can you see, by the dawn's early light,
What so proudly we hailed at the twilight's last gleaming?
Whose broad stripes and bright stars, thru the perilous fight,
O'er the ramparts we watched, were so gallantly streaming?
And the rockets' red glare, the bombs bursting in air,
Gave proof through the night that our flag was still there.
O say, does that star-spangled banner yet wave
O'er the land of the free and the home of the brave?

THE NEGRO NATIONAL ANTHEM-OFFICIAL AFRICAN-AMERICAN NATIONAL HYMN

Lift every voice and sing,
'Til earth and heaven ring,
Ring with the harmonies of Liberty,
Let our rejoicing rise
High as the listening skies,
Let it resound loud as the rolling sea.
Sing a song full of the faith that the dark past has taught
     us,
Sing a song full of the hope that the present has brought
     us,
Facing the rising sun of our new day begun,
Let us march on 'til victory is won.
Stony the road we trod,
Bitter the chast'ning rod.
Felt in the days when hope unborn had died;
Yet with a steady beat,
Have not our weary feet
Come to the place for which our fathers sighed?
We have come, treading our path through the blood of the
     slaughtered,
Out from the gloomy past,
'Til now we stand at last
Where the white gleam of our bright star is cast.
God of our weary years,
God of our silent tears,
Thou who has brought us thus far on the way;
Thou who has by Thy might
Led us into the light,
Keep us forever in the path, we pray
Lest our feet stray from the places, our God, where we met
     Thee,
Lest, our hearts drunk with the wine of the world, we

forget Thee;
Shadowed beneath Thy hand,
May we forever stand,
True to our God,
True to our native land.
James Weldon Johnson   John Rosamond Johnson

GAME KICKOFF TIME =SIGNAL BY THE REFEREE
Half-time Party
6:00 p.m. — Homecoming Dance and After Party
9:00 p.m. — 2:00 a.m. — Students dance and national artist
performs in the gym or in the Stadium

Sunday
10:00 a.m. — Morning Worship Service — Special Hall
2:00 p.m. — Gospel Fest
4:00 P.M. SEND-OFF FOR NEXT YEAR

Psalm 23
1. *The LORD is my shepherd; I shall nor want.*
2. *He maketh me to lie down in green pastures: He leadeth me beside the still waters.*
3. *He restoreth my soul: He leadeth me in the paths of rightousness for his names sake*
4. *Yea, though I walk through the valley of the shadow of death, I will fear no evil: for thou art with me: thy rod and thy staff comfort me*
5. *Thou preparest a table before me in the presence of mine enemies: thou anointest my head with oil; my cup runneth over*
6. *Surely goodness and mercy shall follow me all the days of my life: and I will dwell in the house of the LORD forever.*

WHAT IS TAILGATING?
CIAA

What is Tailgating?

The homecoming football game is one of the biggest games held on HBCUs Historically Black Colleges and Universities (HBCUs) campuses. Celebrations not only include crowning of the homecoming queen and her court, but also with the Alumni staking out prime areas of the campus near the football field designed for tailgaters.

Tailgaters come well equipped with cookers, food, beverages and memorabilia. The grills may be costumed — made or store bought. They may be charcoal, gas or wood. Some are similar to a restaurant on wheels. Most can accommodate up to fifty or more people. The tailgaters menu has a whole gamut of items, such as, barbeque (ribs, beef, chicken) fried fish, grilled corn and many types of drinks. Usually a fine array of music played by a sound system or a boom box of favorite tunes provides hits for the tailgate party.

Homecoming week at the HBCUs Historically Black Colleges and Universities (HBCUs) Campuses is more like a family reunion rather than a culmination of a football game. Activities center on the historical beginning of the colleges and universities up to the future, the incorporation of school and community.

Cars, vans, trucks, motor homes and SUVs make up the tailgating modes of transportation. These vehicles are decorated with the schools stickers, flags and license plates. Tailgating can be seen in designated parts of the campus. Always try to park next to a grassy area or at the end of a parking area. The extra room gives more Partying space.

Tailgating Contents

HBCUs Historically Black Colleges and Universities (HBCUs) Campuses written rules are published a year in advance. Tailgaters may enter contest and run various prizes ranging from trophies, fancy grills up to large monetary prizes. Judges are giving set of rules for grilling food, presentation of tailgate area or of surrounding contest.

Food categories may include: Best Gumbo, Best Barbeque Ribs, Best Fried Fish or Best Philly Steak. All contestants must abide by rules of the contest or they will be disqualified. If the tailgaters enter a cooking contest they must adhere to refrigeration and fire safety, sanitation electrical rules. They must follow county, state or federal rules.

Cleanliness is of utmost when dealing with food. Safety also, is of the utmost. Fire extinguishers must be kept on the scene.

Tailgating Party Menus and Recipes

The themes of the tailgating menus are centered on Georgians who are graduates of Historically Black Colleges and Universities located in Georgia. Products and recipes are given by many of these people. I have extended the recipes so that the servings will be for at least fifty people.

Georgia has a rich agricultural heritage. Tailgating in another way can be seen all over with the farmers and their families selling fresh products off the backs of their pickup trucks alongside the roads, in the markets, on back street, under a shade tree or anywhere possible to offer choices of a wide range of fresh vegetables and fruits and sometimes canned products. There is also several vineyards in Georgia. People make all kinds of wines. Wine making is a home is also a must for many families.

This cookbook on tailgating is just for fun. I have seen many of the tailgaters in action and found them to be very organized and very different.

I will include types of:
◻ Grilling
◻ Food Safety
◻ Types of Equipment commonly used.

SLAVE VIGNETTES

SLAVE SAYINGS:
CHURCH IN THE WOODS

"On des plantation dey did'nt have no regular church for the slaves an' so when de weather wuz good de slaves went to de woods an' had church in a bush=arbor.Dey made a bush by takin' some post an' putting 'tem in de groun' an' coverin' de top wid bushes. Later on dey had a shelter covered wic boards. De prechin' wuz done by a ol' man dey called Caesar-hewuz too olf yo do anything else an' so prechin' wuz de bibis' thing he done.

GOOD ETIQUETTE FOR TAILGATING PARTIES AND FOOD SAFETY

BE SAFE-USE EXTRA CAUTION

CENTRAL INTERCOLLEGIATE ATHLETIC ASSOCIATION (CIAA) OLDEST HISTORICALLY BLACK COLLEGE AND UNIVERSITY DIVISION
Establishment is 1912

NORTHERN DIVISION	SOUTHERN DIVISION
BOWIE STATE UNIVERSITY	FAYETTEVILLE STATE UNIVERSITY
LINCOLN UNIVERSITY	JOHNSON C. SMITH
ELIZABETH CITY UNIVERSITY	LIVINGSTONE COLLEGE
VIRGINIA STATE UNIVERSITY	SAINTAUGUSTINE COLLEGE
VIRGINIA UNION UNIVERSITY	WINSTON-SALEM UNIVERSITY
ST. PAUL'S COLLEGE	SHAW UNIVERSITY

SCHOOL/ LOCATION OF SCHOOL /MASCOT
BOWIE STATE UNIVERSITY BOWIE, MARYLAND, BULLDOGS
ELIZABETH CITY STATE UNIVERSITY ELIZABETH CITY, NORTH CAROLINA VIKINGS
FAYETTE VILLE STATE UNIVERSITY, FAYETTE VILLE, NORTH CAROLINA, BRONCOS
JOHNSON C. SMITH UNIVERSITY, CHARLOTTE, NORTH CAROLINA GOLDEN BULLS

LINCOLN UNIVERSITY, PENNSYLVANIA- LINCOLN UNIVERSITY PENNSYLVANIA - LIONS
LIVINGSTONE COLLEGE- SALISBURY, NORTH CAROLINA-BLUE BEARS ST. AUGUSTINE'S COLLEGE RALEIGH, NORTH CAROLINA -FALCONS
ST. PAUL'S COLLEGE LAWRENCEVILLE, VIRGINIA TIGERS SHAW UNIVERSITY RALEIGH, NORTH CAROLINA BEARS

VIRGINIA STATE UNIVERSITY PETERSBURG, VIRIGINA TROJANS
VIRGINIA UNION UNIVERSITY RICHMOND, VIRGINIA PANTHERS
WINSTON SALEM STATE UNIVERSITY WINSTON SALEM- NORTH CAROLINA- RAMS

GOOD ETIQUETTE FOR TAILGATING
IN GENERAL

-DRAW UP A PLAN, A BUDGET AND AN INVITATION LIST.

-Make a list of items. Check off the list as you pack. Try to pack all nonperishable goods the night before.

-DO NOT PLAY MUSIC TOO LOUDLY OTHERS MAY NOT CARE FOR YOUR MUSIC.

---KEEP SURROUNDINGS CLEAN

WHILE COOKING

-DO NOT EAT FROM COOKING SPOONS OR FORKS, USE TASTING SPOON.

-ALWAYS WASH YOUR HANDS BEFORE COOKING EVEN THOUGH YOU USE GLOVES, WET WIPES, WET DISPOABLE CLOTHS FOR CLEANING HANDS AND SURFACES.

-KEEP HANDY -FIRE EXTINGUISHER, FIRST AID KIT, TRASH BAGS, WATER AND PLENTY OF ICE.

WHEN SERVING

-ALWAYS HAVE PLENTY OF FLATWARE, (SPOONS, KNIVES, FORKS), NAPKINS, PLATES, CUPS, paper towels.

-Always use size of servings

-Keep hot foods hot, and cold foods cold

-DO NOT EAT FROM SERVING UTENSILS OF SERVING CONTAINERS.

SUGGESTED FOOD SAFETY TIPS

Temperatures When Grilling
Keeping Food Hot and Cold

◘ The temperature range to which micro-organisms grow best is referred to as the danger zone 40 degrees to 140 degrees.

◘ The cold food is held below 40 degrees F and hot food is held above 140 degrees F, the risk of contracting a food borne illness is greatly reduced.

◘ Safe holding temperatures for cooked food is 140 degrees and above.

◘ Poultry should not be eaten if it is pink in the center, if the juices are pink, or if the final internal cooking temperatures do not reach 170 degrees F.

◘ Hamburger and other ground meat should be well done and should not be eaten if the final cooking temperatures do not reach 165 degrees F in the center.

◘ A piece of meat such as a steak or roast that has not been pierced during processing or preparation is safe to eat if it reaches an internal temperature of 145 degrees F.

◘ When having a picnic in hot weather (above 85 degree F), put up food quickly and throw away food that has been left out more than an hour.

◘ All leftover cooked foods should be reheated to an internal temperature of 165 degrees F. Do not leave perishable food at room temperature for more than two hours.

◘ Thaw frozen food in the refrigerator or microwave.

Thawing in the refrigerator:

◘ Place the food in or over a dish that will catch thawing liquids and keep them from contaminating other foods in the refrigerator.

• Place thawing food near the bottom of the refrigerator to keep them from contaminating other foods.

Thawing under running water:

◻ Place food, still packaged or wrapped in plastic, in a sink or in a pot in a sink.

◻ Run cold water over food. The water (which could be contaminated) should not be allowed to splash on other foods or surfaces.

◻ Foods may be thawed this way if it takes no more than two hours.

Thawing in the microwave

◻ When you thaw foods in the microwave oven, you are "heating them slowly". The surface will support bacterial growth before the center is thawed.

◻ Immediately after thawing food in the microwave, the food must then be cooked thoroughly. If the thawed warm food is stored instead of cooked, there will be a rapid growth of bacteria.

Food Safety Tips

◻ Follow these safety guidelines for properly thawing, preparing, cooking and storing turkey and its trimming.

◻ Use an accurate meat thermometer when cooking a turkey. When alone, the internal temperature at the thickest part of the thigh should be 180 degrees F to 185 degrees F.

◻ Wash your hands often as you prepare the meal so raw juices don't get on other foods.

◻ Wash utensils, cutting boards, bowls, and other equipment with soap and hot water after contact with turkey.

◻ Don't let raw meat or perishable items stay out of the refrigerator or unheated for more than two hours.

◻ Cook turkey immediately after preparation. Don't let it sit on the counter where dangerous bacteria can grow.

◻ Don't use oven temperatures lower than 325 degrees F.

◻ Store leftovers promptly.

At the Grocery Store

◻ Select meats and poultry last.

◻ Avoid cross contamination and avoid packages that leak if you are not going home directly from the store, use a cooler to keep perishables cold.

◻ Cooked products should not be left unrefrigerated longer than 2 hours.

◻ uI Store raw meat and poultry at or below 40 degrees Fahrenheit.

◻ Never defrost at room temperature. Frozen products should be defrosted in the refrigerator or for quicker thawing in cold running water or in the microwave.

◻ Fresh poultry can be stored in the refrigerator for 1 to 2 days and the freezer for 6 to 9 months cooked poultry can remain in the refrigerator two days.

Food Safety Information and Food Borne Illnesses

Food Borne Illnesses

Definition:
Food borne illness is a disease that is caused by pathogenic micro-organisms in food.

The causes include bacteria, parasites, viruses and molds.

Symptoms:
Bacteria: Bacteria cause most food borne illness. Bacteria can be brought into food for people or raw animal and plant products such as eggs, beef or fresh fruit and vegetables or on trucks, equipment or boxes used to transport food.

Viruses: Viruses use food only as a way to move themselves from one place to another. They may be in seafood or shellfish which is eaten raw. They are also found in contaminated water. Viruses are often passed onto food by an infected person. Good personal hygiene habits can also stop the spreads viruses.

Parasites: Parasites are micro-organisms that survive by living on or inside a host. They are usually found in raw seafood or animal foods. Cook these foods completely will kill the parasites.

Molds: Molds often make toxins that make a person sick or may potentially cause concerns. Foods that have a lot of mold on them should be thrown out.

Symptoms:
Includes nausea, vomiting, diarrhea, stomach pains, chills, and fever, headache and muscle pains.

Sanitation and personal hygiene
Factors that contribute to food borne illnesses are spoiled food, poor personal hygiene, poor sanitation practices, and lack of temperature control and cross contaminants.

Good hygiene is important in the battle against foodborne illness. The most common problems include hand washing, smoking clothing hair, illness and visit to the restroom.

Cleaning removes food and garbage from utensils or work surfaces, while sanitizing lowers the number of micro-organisms to a safe level.

Insects and rodents are unsightly and unsanitary. You should be most concerned about the fact that they can carry diseases. The first line of defense against insects and rodents is to keep the area clean and sanitary.

Avoid Cross-Contamination

Cross-contamination is the transfer of pathogenic micro-organisms from one food or food contact to another food. The following are a few guidelines to promote sanitation and prevent cross contamination.

- Wash hands before preparing or eating and after handling raw meat, poultry or fish. Wash hands during food preparation, you touch hair, cough, sneeze, blow nose or contaminate hands in other ways.
- Keep refrigerator and kitchen clean and wipe up spills immediately. Store raw meat, poultry or fish on a plate, in a plastic bag, or fish thoroughly before using them again for cooked food.
- Never reuse a cutting board after cutting raw meat, poultry, or fish without first thoroughly washing cutting board.
- Use clean plates, glasses and utensils when eating or preparing food.
- Keep sink, countertops, appliances and tables clean.
- Never reuse plastic food storage bags.

Time and Temperature Guidelines

- Keep cold foods cold and hot foods hot when preparing, serving and eating food. Put food away as soon as possible and never leave food, drinks at room temperature for more than two hours.

- Reheat leftovers to 165 degrees F and bring leftover souses to a rolling boil.
- Refrigerate mayonnaise, ketchup, and salad dressing as soon as they are opened.
- Make sure the temperature of the refrigerator is 40 F or below and freezer or below.
- Never leave groceries in a hot car, put them away immediately.
- Never eat half-cooked eggs or foods that contain raw eggs.

Safety tips for chicken

- Cooked chicken refrigerate for 3 to 4 days and in the freezer four months.
- Wash hands, surfaces including boards before and after preparing or handling raw meat and poultry.
- Use and then discard towels to wipe up raw meat and poultry juices.
- Wash sponges and dishtowels often.
- Do not reuse marinade. Before you marinate meat, set aside extra marinade if you want to use it on cooked dish.
- Use a clean platter to serve cooked food not the same one used to hold uncooked food.
- Cook chicken properly to kill bacteria. Juices should not run clear, or pink.
- Whole chicken should be cooked to 189 degrees F; one-in parts to 170.
- Degrees boneless parts, to 160 degrees. Use meat thermometer and always measure at the thickest part.
- Place leftovers in shallow dishes and refrigerate or freeze promptly.
- Pack lunches/picnics in insulated carriers with a cold pack. Never leave lunches in direct sun or on a warm radiator.
- When grilling out, clean the grill before each use to prevent bacteria contamination.

Storing Catfish in the Freezer

◘ Remove skin from the fillet with a super sharp knife.

◘ Always cut out the bones before packing away.

◘ Vacuum sealing can be used for store and freeze.

◘ Wipe any excess water or blood from fillet with paper towel; then individually wrap fillet willet in plastic, squeezing air out before sealing completely.

◘ After freezing allow a day to thaw in refrigerator before using.

◘ Before cooking trim any freezer bum portions away.

Most Popular Germ Hangouts

◘ The kitchen sink — perhaps the dirtiest place within the house, guzzles down million of germs daily from raw meat, fish, fruits and veggies.

◘ Sponges harbor millions of germs within their tiny pores because they provided a moist, dark and warm environment that most sink germs crave.

◘ Countertops harbor germs even if they look clean — some germs can live for hours to days on dry surfaces.

◘ Cutting boards, either plastic or wood, have the kind of cracks and crevices that raw meat and veggies — germs love to hide in.

◘ Doorknobs and handles, like the one on your refrigerator, attract viruses and bacteria from every hand in the house.

◘ Tubs and showers not only have viruses and bacteria, but they're often filled with mold and milder, too.

◘ Hand towels breed millions of germs daily because of their frequent shared use.

◘ Computer keyboards are rampant with germs, particularly if you eat while you type.

◘ Pets are cute and fluffy but frequent carriers of all kinds of germs and diseases, including those that come from worms, ticks and fleas.

How can you protect yourself and your family? Regularly clean all sinks, countertops and doorknobs with a commercial cleanser or a mild bleach solution. Disinfect sponges and cutting boards in your dishwasher and limit tea towels to a one time use per person or use paper towels. Use alcohol pads to quickly clean computer keys. Keep pets free of worms, ticks and fleas.

Proper hand washing — wet your hands, add soap, and rub them together for 20 seconds, then rinse well. Use a paper towel to dry your hands. When you get the urge to sneeze, do so in a tissue or in your sleeve to help prevent germs from spreading.

Sanitation and Personal Hygiene
Factors that contribute to food borne illnesses are spoiled food, poor personal hygiene, poor sanitation practices, and lack of temperature control and cross contamination.

Good hygiene is important in the battle against food borne illness. The most common problems include hand washing, smoking, clothing, hair, illness and visit to the restroom.

Contamination of food can come from humans, as well as, unclean utensils, equipment and work surfaces.

Cleaning removes food and garbage from utensils or work surfaces, while sanitizing lowers the number of micro-organisms to a safe level.

Insects and rodents are unsightly and unsanitary. You should be most concerned about the fact that they carry diseases. The first line of defense against insects and rodents (pests) is to keep the area clean and sanitary.

Storing Foods Safely
- Food received in good condition can only remain in good condition if it is stored under the best condition.
- Poor storage practices can lead to early spoilage of a food.
- Always follow the first in, first out rule (FIFO).
- Date incoming foods so that you know which are the oldest and use those products first when storing food

in the refrigerator or freezer, packaging must be intact and air tight.

◻ Large quantities of food cannot be cooked rapidly in a holding refrigerator, pre-chill or divide into small portions.

◻ Store raw, uncooked foods on the bottom of the refrigerator, prepared foods on top.

◻ When storing food in the freezer, be sure to arrange in ways that help air to circulate around food, allowing for quicker freezing.

◻ Store food in a way that prevents spoilage by molds, insects, rodents or moisture.

Storing Perishable Food Safely

◻ Keep refrigerator at 34 F to 40 for lower.

◻ Remove spoiled food and clean refrigerator surfaces regularly.

◻ Separate cooked and raw food, wrap food properly and refrigerate leftovers immediately.

◻ Use raw meat promptly and pay attention to the "sell by" dates and other fresh food.

◻ Preheat frozen cooked food without thawing.

When in doubt, throw it out

Remember, when in doubt about food that looks, smells and tastes good, throw it out. Contaminated food may look good enough to eat, but can be deadly.

Types of Grills
Grills, equipment, tools have all been used by tailgaters

1. Char-Griller Smoker
   Outdoor Smoker
   - A 1,000 square grill area
   - Cast iron cooking grates
   - With adjustable charcoal grade height for temperature control with side fire box (cost approximate $149.00)
2. Outdoor Gourmet Walnut —Finished Island Grill with Stainless Steel "U" burners,, 54,000 — BUT
   - Infrared back burner 1 2000-BTU
   - 810— sq. inch of total cooking space
   - 304 stainless firebox, cooking grates and heat diffuses
   - Granite countertops
   - Includes ice chest, smoke drawer, rotisserie kit
   - i.e., without cracks in the grill, old spills or broken gas lens.
   - Do not forget to get new gas before going o a trip

Packing up your Grill
- Carry plenty of trash bags — larger bags.
- Carefully clean grill, destroy all fire sources.
- Refrigerate useable ingredients.
- Place trash in designated place.
- Make a list of cleanup procedures.
- Properly store items. Do take your time.

Equipment - Grills
Outdoor Gourmet Three-Burner Gas Grill with Side Burner - $200.00
- Three stainless steel burners.
- 36,000 total BTU
- 12,000 BTU Side Burner
- 620 sq in. total cooking area

Blackstone Griddle - $299.00
- Four independent Burners
- Large 36 in. width cooking surface
- Folding legs make it easily transportable

Brinkman Smoke N' Grill — $34.99
- Double-grill charcoal smoker with burnt in heat indicator

Char-Griller Patro Pro - $69.99
- 250 sq. in. grill area

1. Dual-Zone Charcoal Grill
   - Dual cooking zones with adjustable charcoal trays — fully enclosed storage cabinet.

2. Char-Griller Smokin — Outlaw - $179.00
   Smoker — 1000 sq. in. area
   - Cast iron cooking grates
   - Wood cooking — 179.

3. Oklahoma Joes Longhorn Smoker - $49.00
   - Heavy — gauged skill
   - Over 900 sq. in. cooking surface
   - Slide-out ash drawer

4. Brinkman Island — Style Gas Grill
   - Four stainless steel burners, 48,000 BTU total
   - 13,500 BTU cast iron side burner
   - Porcelain — coated cast iron grate
   - 760 sq. in. of total cooking surface.

Tailgating Equipment and Supplies

1. Outdoor Gourmet Lee 11 — piece combo Fryer Kit - $69.00
2. Outdoor Gourmet Stainless Steel Turkey Fryer Kit - $89.99.
3. Power Carver for carving meat ˙
4. Comfortable Armchairs - $6.99
5. Over-sized Aluminum Armchairs
6. Coolers — Select a variety.
7. Large Pots —10 GALLON POTS, LARGE IRON BLACK POTS
8. Cooking Utensils - Stirring spoons, tongs, spatulas, butcher knives, chef knives
9. Paper Goods — One case each paper towels, napkins, flatware, cups -20 ounces,
10. Tablecloths - Plastic or Paper

TAILGATING ESSENTIALS

1. CANOPY or POP-UP TENT
2. TABLE AND CHAIRS
3. Plenty of Ice and Ice coolers
4. Timber Creek Stove or Grills
5. Plenty of Paper goods and Food
6. Cookers and fuel source
7. Night lights
8. Port —a- Potty,
9. RV OR SUV OR PREFERENCE IN CARS OR TRUCKS
10. MUSIC, TELEVISON, GAMES AND OF COURSE, THE PEOPLE

SUGGESTIONS FOR SELECTING A GRILL
◘ Determine what you will cook.
◘ Be sure to learn how to operate grill before you tailgate.
◘ Learn all of the safety rules of cooking week your personal grill.
◘ Learn proper maintenance and storage of a grill for travel.

Traveling with a Grill
◘ Be sure to carry a fire extinguisher and plenty of water.
◘ Carry baking soda.
◘ Pack grill carefully in especially if your source of heat is propane or wood.
◘ Test your grill before use to ensure that it is in good working conditions.

CENTRAL INTERCOLLEGIATE ATHLETIC ASSOCIATION NORTHERN DIVISION

NORTHERN CIAA

Bowie State University
Bowie, Maryland

Motto: "Prepare for Life"

History: 1865 (Founded in 1865, Public, 3581/2 acres)

Enrollment: 5,483

Degrees Granted: 20 undergraduate, 20 masters programs and 2 doctoral programs

School Colors: Blue and Gold

Nickname/Mascots: Bulldogs

Name of Band: Bowie State Marching Band

Name of Stadium: Bulldog Stadium

Sports: Basketball (m&w), bowling, cross-country, football, indoor track and field (m&w), outdoor track and field (m&w), softball, tennis (m&w), volleyball

Classic BOWL Games Classics 5th Prince George Classic Bowie State vs. Lincoln of Penn

Lincoln University
Pennsylvania

Motto: "If the Son shall make you free ye shall be free indeed."

Name of School: Lincoln University

History: Founded 1854 (state school ,422 acres)

Enrollment: 2500

Degrees granted: undergradate and graduate degree

Name of Marching Band: Lincoln University Marching Band

Name of Stadium: Avon Grove High School (Temporary)

♦ ♦ ♦

Sports: Football, cross-country (m&w), basketball, golf, track & field, baseball, tennis

(m&w), softball, bowling

Classic Football Game: 1) ANNUAL ST. PRINCE GEORGE Bowie State vs. Lincoln of Penn

Elizabeth City State University
Elizabeth City, North Carolina

Motto: "To Live is to Learn"

History: Founded 1891 (Public, 200 acres)

ENROLLMENT: 2,500

DEGREES GRANTED: Baccalaureate and Masters

School Colors: Royal Blue and White

Nickname: Mascot: Vikings

Name of Band: Elizabeth City State Marching Band

Name of Stadium: Roebuck Stadium

Sports: Basketball, Cross-country Track, tennis, track & field, softball, football

Classic Bowl Games: 11th Down East Viking Football Classic Elizabeth City State University- Rocky Mount, North Carolina

St. Paul's College
Lawrenceville, VA

Name of School: Saint Paul's College

Date Established: 1888

School Colors: Orange and Black

Nickname/Mascot: Tigers

Name of Band: St. Paul's College Marching Band

Name of Stadium: St. Paul's Athletic Field

Sports: Basketball (m&w), baseball, softball, cross-country, football, track and field

(m&w), golf, tennis (m&w), bowling, volleyball

Classic Football Game: 7th Annual Lucille M. Brown Community Youth Bowl 73rd Annual Classic Virginia Union vs. St. Paul's College

Shaw University
Raleigh, North Carolina

Motto: Pro Christo Est. Humanitate - For Christ and Humanity

History: Founded 1865 (Private-Social Research Institution — Urban campus)

Enrollment: 2800

Degrees Granted: Baccalaureate and Master degrees

School Colors: Maroon and White

Nickname/ Mascot: Bears

Name of Band: Platinum Sound

Name of Stadium: Durham County Stadium

Sports: Football, basketball,

CLASSIC BOWL GAMES: 1) CAPITAL CITY CLASSIC

Texas Southern vs Shaw —Sacramento, California

● ● ●

Virginia State University
Petersburg, VA

MOTTO: "Dream, Explore, Succeed"

History: Founded 1882, Public -land-grant, suburban, 236 acres)

Enrollment: 5,000 students

School Colors: Blue and Orange

Nickname/Mascot: Trojans

Degrees Granted: Bachelors and Masters degrees

Name of Band: Virginia State Trojan Explosion Marching Band

Name of Stadium: Rogers Stadium

Sports: Golf, football, baseball, bowling, volleyball, cross-country, tennis, basketball,

Virginia Union University
Richmond, VA

History: 1865(Private, Urban, 84 acres, American Baptist Church Affiliation)

ENROLLMENT: 1,578

DEGREES GRANTED: Baccalaureate and master degrees

School Colors: Maroon and Steel

Nickname/Mascot: Panthers

Name of Band: Virginia Union Marching Band

Name of Stadium: Hovey Field

Sports: Softball, volleyball, cross-country (m&w), basketball (m&w), track and field (m&w), baseball, tennis (m&w), bowling

SLAVE VIGNETTES

SLAVE SAYINGS

"Although the Emancipation Proclamation was delivered on January 1863, it was not until Lee's final surrender that most of the negroes knew they were free. The Freedman's Bureau in Augusta gave out the news officially to the negroes but in most cases the plantation owners themselves summoned their slaves and told them they were free. Many negroes stayed right with the masters."

"Carrie Lewis, a slave on Captain Ward's plantation in Richmond County, said, when asked where she went when freedom came "Ma? I didn't went nowhere. De niggers come 'long wid de babies and dey back and say I was free, and I tell 'em I was free already. Didn't make no diffunce to me-freedom".

Ex-Slave Carrie Lewis

GEORGIA TAILGATERS MENUS

SOUTHERN DIVISION OF CIAA

The Central Intercollegiate Athletic Association established in 1912 is the nation's oldest black athletic conference.

SOUTHERN DIVISION

    Fayetteville State University
    Johnson C. Smith
    Livingston College
    Saint Augustine College
    Winston-Salem University

Georgia Tailgaters and Georgia Recipes

The tailgaters and recipes represent the Georgia tailgaters, their choice of recipes, many Georgia products and some Georgia people's method of making homecoming spirits and menus.

Suggested Tailgating Menus*

Georgia Agronomist — Tailgater Number 1
Appetizers
Fried Green Tomatoes
Entrée
Pepperoni Pizza
Dessert
Pound Cake
Homecoming Spirit
Green Apple Wine

Air Force Pilot — Tailgater Number 2
Appetizers
Marinated Cherry Tomatoes
Entrée
Smoked Baron of Beef
Dessert
Coconut Patties
Homecoming Spirit
Strawberry/Grape Wine

Georgia Biologists — Tailgater Number 3
Appetizer
Souse Meat
Entrée
Baby Back Ribs
Dessert
Black Berry Cobbler

Homecoming Spirits
Cantaloupe Wine

Airman — Tailgater Number 4
Appetizer
Fried Chicken Necks
Entrée
Chinese Barbeque
Dessert
Bread Pudding
Homecoming Spirit
Apple/Grape Wine

Georgia Banker — Tailgater Number 5
Appetizer
Barbeque Pig's Feet
Entrée
Grilled Pork Loin Chops
Dessert
Peanut Butter Cookies
Homecoming Spirits
Strawberry/Peach Wine

Georgia Cardiologists — Tailgater Number 6
Appetizer
Crab Salad
Entrée
Grilled Sirloin Steak
Dessert
Watermelon Slices
Homecoming Spirits
Purple Plum Wine

Georgia Caseworker — Tailgater Number 7
Appetizer
Vegetable Medley Kabobs

Entrée
Grilled Crab Cakes
Dessert
Grilled Cantaloupes Slices
Homecoming Spirit
Mayhaw Grape Wine

Georgia Chemist — Tailgater Number 8
Appetizer
Baby Carrots/Celery Sticks/Ranch Dressing Dipping Sauce
Entrée
Grilled Lamb Chops
Dessert
S'Mores
Homecoming Spirits
Strawberry/Kiwi Wine

Georgia Cook — Tailgater Number 9
Appetizer
Pickled Okra/Cherry Kabobs
Entrée
Grilled Skinless Chicken Breast
Dessert
Chocolate Covered Donuts
Homecoming Spirits
Plum Wine

Georgia Counselor — Tailgater Number 10
Appetizer
Cheddar Cheese Kabobs
Entrée
Baby Back Ribs
Dessert
Grilled Pear Slices
Homecoming Spirits
Cherry/Nectarine Wine

Georgia Court Clerk — Tailgater Number 11
Appetizer
Red Beans/Hot Cheese Dip
Entrée
Whole Hog Barbeque
Dessert
Cherry Cobbler
Homecoming Spirits
Wild Ranch/Plum Wine

Georgia Choir Director — Tailgater Number 12
Appetizer
Avocado Dip/Chips
Entrée
Grilled Smoked Sausage Links
Dessert
Coconut Miniatures Pies
Homecoming Spirits
Strawberry Wine

Georgia Democrat — Tailgater Number 13
Appetizer
Black-Eyed Peas Caviar/Chips
Entrée
Smoked Turkey
Dessert
Raisin Bread Pudding
Homecoming Spirits
Elderberry Wine

Georgia Dentist — Tailgater Number 14
Appetizer
Fried Spanish Peanuts
Entrée
Barbequed Short Ribs

Dessert
Caramel Apples
Homecoming Spirits
Muscadine Grape Wine

Georgia Doctor of Oncology — Tailgater Number 15
Appetizer
Extra Hot Wings
Entrée
Smoked Beef Brisket
Dessert
Chocolate Krispies
Homecoming Spirits
Pear Wine

Georgia Entomologist — Tailgater Number 16
Appetizer
Hallelujah Dip
Entrée
Jerk Chicken Drummettes
Dessert
Chess Pie Tarts
Homecoming Spirits
Apricot Wine

Georgia Farmer — Tailgater Number 17
Appetizer
Barbequed Goat Kabobs
Entrée
Breakfast Salmon Croquettes/Cheese Grits
Dessert
Candied Apples
Homecoming Spirits
Peach Wine

Georgia Funeral Director — Tailgater Number 18
Appetizer
Kentucky Burgoo Stew
Entrée
Barbequed Chicken Quarters
Dessert
Kentucky Bourbon Pecan Cake
Homecoming Spirits
Wild Grape/ Plum Wine

Georgia General Scientist — Tailgater Number 19
Appetizer
Roasted Goober Peanuts
Entrée
Barbequed Country — Style Pork Ribs
Dessert
Sweet Potato Pie
Homecoming Spirits
Sweet Potato Wine

Georgia Hair Stylists — Tailgater Number 20
Appetizer
Grilled Sweet Potatoes
Entrée
Barbeque Pulled Pork
Dessert
Strawberry Shortcake
Homecoming Spirits
Apple/Cherry Wine

Georgia Horticulturist — Tailgater Number 21
Appetizer
Marinated Broccoli Spears
Entrée
Barbeque Pulled Beef

Dessert
Peanut Crumble
Homecoming Spirits
Scuppernong/Strawberry Wine

Georgia Industrial Engineer — Tailgater Number 22
Appetizer
Smoked Almond Snacks
Entrée
Smoked Salmon Fillets
Dessert
Cherry Nut Cobbler
Homecoming Spirits
Kiwi Wine

Georgia Family and Consumer Scientist Educator Tailgater Number 23
Appetizer
Assorted Fruit Kabobs
Entrée
Spaghetti Meat Sauce Grilled Garlic Bread
Dessert
Goat Milk Peach Ice Cream
Homecoming Spirits
Strawberry/Persimmons Wine

Georgia Fisherman — Tailgater Number 24
Appetizer
Boiled Spicy Peanuts
Entrée
Boiled Crabs Legs
Dessert
Grilled Honey Buns
Homecoming Spirits
Peach /Mulberry/ Grape Wine

Georgia House Planner — Number 25
Appetizer
She Crab Soup
Entrée
Virginia Chopped Ham
Dessert
Popcorn Balls
Homecoming Spirits
Corn Wine

House Representative — Tailgater Number 26
Appetizer
Spicy Chicken Gizzard
Entrée
Shrimp Po' Boys
Dessert
Apple Cobbler
Homecoming Spirit
Green Plum Wine

House Husband — Tailgater Number 27
Appetizer
Fried Chicken Livers
Entrée
Grilled Gulf Shrimp Kabobs
Dessert
Coconut/Pecan/Walnut Tarts
Homecoming Spirits
Apricot Wine

Infant and Child Developmentalist — Tailgater Number 28
Appetizer
Salsa and Chips
Entrée
Tacos

Dessert
Apple Fried Pies
Homecoming Spirits
Strawberry /Papaya Wine

Georgia Informer — Tailgate Number 29

Appetizer
Nachos
Entrée
Grilled Pork Chops
Dessert
Strawberry Torte
Homecoming Spirits
Blackberry/ Green Apple Wine

Georgia Information Specialist — Tailgater Number 30

Appetizer
Popcorn Chicken
Entréc
Barbeque Beef Ribs
Dessert
Grilled Chocolate Nut Krisp
Homecoming Spirits
Apple/Cinnamon Wine

Georgia GBI — Tailgater Number 31

Appetizer
Deep Fried Onion Blossoms
Entrée
Grilled T-Bone Steak
Dessert
Fried Apple Pies
Homecoming Spirits
Post Oak Grape Wine

Georgia Jailer — Tailgater Number 32
Appetizer
> Deep Fried Pretzels

Entrée
> Grilled Sirloin Steaks

Desserts
> Graham Crackers/Marshmallows

Homecoming Spirits
> Concord Grape Wine

Georgia Farmer — Tailgater Number 33
Appetizer
> Baked Sweet Potatoes

Entrée
> Grilled Kansas City Strips

Dessert
> Grilled Peach Halves

Homecoming Spirits
> Cherry Lime Wine

Georgia Lawyer Tailgater Number 34
Appetizer
> Fresh Purple Plums

Entrée
> Grilled Hamburgers

Dessert
> Baklava

Homecoming Spirits
> Muscadine /Mango Wine

Georgia Judge — Tailgater Number 35
Appetizer
> Hushpuppies

Entrée
> Deep Fried Catfish/Collard Greens

Dessert
Grilled Honey Buns
Homecoming Spirits
Apricot/Peach Wine

Georgia Newspaper Reporter — Tailgater Number 36
Appetizer
Tennessee Chicken
Entrée
Memphis Barbeque
Dessert
Oatmeal Cookies
Homecoming Spirits
Crab Apple Wine

Georgia Math Teacher Tailgater Number 37
Appetizer
Syrup Biscuits
Entrée
Frog Legs
Dessert
Banana Split Pie
Homecoming Spirits
Peach Cranberry Wine

Georgia Coach — Tailgater Number 38
Appetizer
Fried Drummettes
Entrée
Pork Chop Sandwiches
Dessert
Walnut Tarts
Homecoming Spirits
Nectarine Wine

Georgia Radio Personality — Tailgater Number 39
Appetizer
Doritos Chips/Avocado Dip
Entrée
Smoked Sausage Links
Dessert
Coconut Tarts
Homecoming Spirits
Strawberry Wine

Georgia Republican — Tailgater Number 40
Appetizer
Pig Skins
Entrée
Barbeque Goat
Dessert
Cinnamon Apple Crunch
Homecoming Spirits
Musk Melon Wine

Georgia Physical Education Teacher Number 41
Appetizers
Teriyaki Wings
Entrée
Fried Alligator Tails
Dessert
Chocolate Pound Cake
Homecoming Spirits
Dew berry Wine

Georgia School Board Member — Tailgater Number 42
Appetizer
Buffalo Chicken Wings
Entrée
Shared Smithfield Ham on Buns

Dessert
Brownies
Homecoming Spirits
Honeydew Wine

Georgia Secretary — Tailgater Number 43

Appetizer
Corn Dogs
Entrée
Sliced Barbeque Pork Butt
Dessert
Brownies
Homecoming Spirits
Rome Beauty Apple Wine

Georgia Space Worker — Tailgater Number 44

Appetizer
Cheese Dip with Apples
Entrée
Fried Chicken Halves
Dessert
Banana Raspberry Tart
Homecoming Spirits
Pear/Wild Grape Wine

Georgia Specialist — Tailgater Number 45

Appetizer
Barbeque Cocktail Smokies
Entrée
Grilled Philly Cheese Sandwich
Dessert
Peanut Butter Cookies
Homecoming Spirits
Raspberry/Strawberry Wine

Georgia Sportscaster — Tailgater Number 46
Appetizer
Popcorn Shrimp
Entrée
Fried Turkey Legs
Dessert
Roasted Marshmallows
Homecoming Spirits
Bing Cherry Wine

Georgia Sound Man — Tailgater Number 47
Appetizer
Grilled Potatoes
Entrée
Grilled Lamb Loin Chops
Dessert
Key Lime Cake
Homecoming Spirits
Peach/Blackberry Wine

Georgia Superintendent — Tailgater Number 48
Appetizer
Deep Fried Jalapenos
Entrée
Whiting Fillets
Dessert
Pumpkin Tarts
Homecoming Spirits
Peach/Grape Bland Wine

Georgia Store Owner-Tailgater Number 49
Appetizers
Popcorn and Peanuts
Entrée
Grilled Steak on a Stick

Dessert
Banana Nut Muffins
Homecoming Spirits
Granny Apple Wine

Georgia Navy Aircraft Pilot — Number 50
Appetizer
Cheese Grits Casserole
Entrée
Fried Talapia
Dessert
Fried Apples Pies
Homecoming Spirits
Delicious Apple Wine

* —All recipes are not included,

SLAVE VIGNETTES

EX-SLAVE

SLAVE RATIONS

"The amount of food given each slave was also inadequate was a general rule. At the end of each week they all went to a certain spot on the plantation where each was given 1 peck of meal, 1 gallon of syrup and 3 pounds of meat. They often suffered from the particular stomach ailment commonly known as hunger. At such times, raids were mad on the smokehouse. This was considered as stealing by the master and the overseer but to them it was merely taking that which they had worked for. At other times they increased their food by hunting and fishing. Possums and coons were the usual game from such a hunting expedition. All meals usually considered of grits, bacon, syrup, corn bread and vegetables. On Sundays and holidays the meals varied to the extent that they were allowed to have biscuits which they called "cake bread". The slaves made coffee by parching corn meal, okra seed or Irish potatoes. When sufficiently parched any one of the above named would make a vile type of coffee. Syrup was used for sweetening purposes. The produce from the gardens which the master allowed could only be used for home consumption and under no circumstances could any be sold."

Ex-Slave

SOUTHERN DIVISION of the CENTRAL INTERCOLLEGIATE ATHLETIC ASSOCIATION

Name of School	Location	Nickname
Fayetteville State University	Fayetteville, North Carolina	Broncos
Johnson C. Smith	Charleston, North Carolina	Golden Bulls
Livingstone	Salisbury, North Carolina	Blue Bears
Saint Augustine	Raleigh, North Carolina	Falcons
Shaw	Raleigh, North Carolina	Bears
Winston Salem State	Winston Salem, North Carolina	Rams

Fayetteville State University
Fayetteville, North Carolina

Name of School: Fayetteville State University

Motto: Res Non Verba — Deeds not words

History: Founded 1867 (Public, 200 acres)

ENROLLMENT: 6,200

DEGREES GRANTED: 44 baccalaureate, 24 masters and one doctorate

School Colors: White and Blue

Nickname: Mascot: Broncos

Name of Stadium: Luther "Nick" Jeralds Stadium

NAME OF MARCHING BAND: Fayetteville State Marching Band

Sports: Basketball, bowling(w), football, golf (m), softball (w), volleyball, cheerleading, cross-country, running, track and field

CLASSIC BOWL GAMES:

Johnson C. Smith
Charlotte, North Carolina

Name of School: Johnson C. Smith University
Motto: Sit Lux — Let There Be Light

History: Founded in 1867

ENROLLMENT: 2,000 +

DEGREES GRANTED: 20 Baccalaureates

School Colors: Gold and Navy Blue

Nickname/ Mascot: Golden Bulls

Name of Band: Johnson C. Smith Marching Band

Name of Stadium: Irwin Belk Complex

Sports: Basketball, bowling, cross-country,, football, golf, softball, tennis (m&w). track and field (m&w)

CLASSIC BOWL GAMES:1) Western Virginia Educators Classic Virginia Union University vs. Johnson C. Smith @Salem

2) COMMEMORATIVE BOWL GAME Johnson C. Smith vs Livingstone College

Livingstone College
Salisbury, North Carolina

Motto: A Call to Commitment: Taking Livingstone College to the next level.

History: Founded 1879 (Private, 272 acres, African Methodist Episcopal Zion Church)

ENROLLMENT: 1,100

DEGREES GRANTED: Bachelor of Arts, Bachelor of Science, Bachelor of Fine Arts, Bachelor of Social Work degrees.

School Colors: Columbia Blue and Black

Nickname: Mascot: Blue Bears

Name of Band: Livingstone Marching Band

Name of Stadium: Alumni Memorial Stadium

Sports: Basketball (m&w), bowling (w), cross-country (m&w), football, softball, volleyball, tennis (m&w), track and field (m&w)

Classic Bowl Games: 1) The Commemorative Classic

Johnson C. Smith vs. Livingstone College

● ● ●

2) GREENVILLE HISTORICALLY BLACK COLLEGES AND UNIVERSITES

Livingstone College vs Concordia College @Greenville

Saint Augustine's College
Raleigh, North Carolina

Motto: Veritas Vos Liberabit — The truth will set you free

History: **Founded** 1867 (Urban, 105 acres, Private)

ENROLLMENT: 1750

DEGREES GRANTED: UNDERGRADUATES

School Colors: Blue and White

Nickname: Mighty Falcons

Name of Band: Saint Augustine's College Marching Band

Name of Stadium: Capital Stadium

Sports: Golf, football, baseball, bowling (m&w), volleyball, cross-country (m&w), tennis (m&w), basketball (m&w), outdoor track (m&w), indoor track (m&w)

CLASSIC BOWL GAMES:

SLAVE VIGNETTES

Slave Sayings

"Tom from the plantation in Virginia remembers distinctly when freedom came to his people. "When we wus about to have freedom" he said, "they thought the Yankees was a-goin' to take all the slaves so they put us on trains and run us down south. I went to a place whut they call 'Butler'

Railroad, then to Quincy, then to Tallahassee. When the war ended

I weren't "xactly in 'Gusta, I was in Irwinville, where they caut Mars. Jeff Davis. Folks said he had de money train, but I never seed no gold, nor

Nobody what had an. I come on up to'Gusta and jined de Bush Arbor."

Ex-Slave Tom

APPETIZERS/SIAC

SOUTHERN INTERCOLLEGIATE ATHLETIC CONFERENCE (SIAC)
1913

ALBANY STATE - ALBANY GA, GOLDEN RAMS

BENEDICT COLLEGE - COLUMBIA SC, BC TIGERS

CLARK - ATLANTA, ATLANTA PANTHERS

FORT VALLEY STATE UNIVERSITY - FORT VALLEY GA, WILDCATS

LANE COLLEGE - JACKSON, TENN DRAGONS

MILES - FAIRFIELD ALA, GOLDEN BEARS

MOREHOUSE COLLEGE - ATLANTA, MAROON TIGERS

KENTUCKY STATE UNIVERSITY - FRANKFORT KENTUCKY, THOROBREDS

STILLMAN COLLEGE - TUSCALOOSA AL, TIGERS

TUSKEGEE - TUSKEGEE AL, GOLDEN TIGERS

Suggested Tailgating Appetizer Recipes

1. Meats
   -Beef, chicken, pork, fish, nuts and soups.
2. Fruits and Vegetables
3. Dairy
4. Soups
   - Stews and others
5. Nuts

Hallelujah Dip

Number of servings 50; Size of servings- 1/4 cup, 5 chips

Amount   Ingredients

15 pounds hamburger meat

4 large yellow onions chopped

10 pounds Velveeta cheese, grated

5 cans (15 ounces Rotel) Tomatoes

10 large bags Doritos Chips

Directions

1. Brown of hamburger meat. Discard fat. Add onions. Stir well. Cook until onions are clear.
2. Pour into large pot. Mix in remaining ingredients. Stir and cook for 1 hour.
3. Serve with chips.

Nachos

Number of servings: 50; size of servings; 1/2 cup serving over 10 chips.

5 cups onions, diced

5 cups green pepper, diced

3 Tablespoons cooking oil

10 pounds Hamburger meat1 tablespoon salt

1 1/2 cups Nacho seasoning

5 large bags tortilla chips

5 pounds medium flavored Cheddar cheese, grated

1 quart jalepeno peppers, sliced

1 quart salsa

Directions

1. Prepare vegetables. Cook in cooking oil until tender. Add hamburger meat; Cook pink leaves meat. Add salt and nacho seasoning. Cook until done. Drain.
2. On a paper tray, place 10 chips, then 1/2 cup meat on top of chips.
3. Top with grated cheese, peppers and salsa. Serve.

Barbeque Hot Link Sausage on a Stick

Number of servings 50; size of servings 1 per person

Amount   Ingredients

10 pounds Beef hot link sausages

50 wooden skewers, soaked in water

1 gallon barbeque sauce

50 hoagie buns

Directions

1. Wash hot links. Put skewers into hot links. Wrap individually with aluminum foil.
2. Grill for 15-20 minutes. Heat barbeque sauce in separate pan on top of grill.
3. To serve, remove foil and dip individual link in sauce using sticks. Serve on buns.

Cocktail Smokies

Number of servings 50; Size of servings 4 sausages per person

Amount   Ingredients

1 gallon commercial barbeque sauce

2 quarts grape jelly

25 pounds cocktail wieners

Directions

1. In a large stock pot, mix together barbeque sauce and grape jelly. Stir well. Heat up on grill and cook to simmer. Add cocktail wieners. Cook for Thirty minutes or until wieners are thoroughly done. Do not overcook.
2. Serve with toothpicks.

Barbeque Pork Riblets

Number of servings 50; size of servings 4 on a sandwich

Amount Ingredients

30 pounds pork riblets, cut into fours

2 pounds seasoning salt

Directions

1. Wash and season ribs and refrigerate for two hours.
2. Grill for 2 hours until done.
3. Soak in barbeque sauce.
4. Serve on buns.

Barbeque Pig's Feet

Number of servings: 50; Size of servings: 1 per person

Amount	Ingredients
50	pig's feet
10	bay leaves
6 cups	yellow onions, chopped
1/4 cup	seasoning salt
2 gallons	commercial barbeque sauce

Directions

1. In three large stock pots, divide pig's feet and cover with water. Distribute bay ;eaves among pots, three to

four per pot and add onions. Boil until very tender. lest with a fork.

2. Drain pig's feet. Discard onions and bay leaves. Cool. Season with seasoning salt.
3. Place in three large aluminum pans. Pour sauce over feet and cook on grill for 30 minutes.
4. Serve on plates; 1 per person.

Pickled Pig's Feet

Number of Servings; 50, Size of servings: one per person.

Amount   Ingredients

50   Pig's feet, clean and hair removed

4 gallons white vinegar + 1 gallon water

4bay leaves

1/2 cup allspice

1/2 cup salt

3 cups sugar

Directions

1. Clean pig's feet, wash and divide into 3 groups. Boil each group three pots of water Boil each pot for 2 hours or until tender. Drain. Set aside.
2. To make vinegar, in a large container, add vinegar, water, bay leaves, allspice, salt and sugar. Stir well. Boil for ten minutes.
3. Pour over pig's feet and cover over night. Serve.

Tennessee Chicken

Number of servings 50; Size of servings; 2 slices

Amount   Ingredients

25 pounds salt pork, cut into 3"X 2" slices

3 gallons water

1 gallon peanut oil

Directions

1. Prepare meat as directed.
2. Boil in water for 15 minutes. Drain. Pat dry.
3. Fry in peanut oil until crispy. Drain. Serve.

Grilled Goat Kabobs

Number of servings -50; size of servings - 1 kabob

Amount   Ingredients

4 goat shoulders, cut into 2 inch cubes

1 gallon cider vinegar

1/2 cup each black pepper, seasoning salt, cumin

12 green bell peppers cut into 1 inch squares

12 yellow onions, quartered

50 wooden skewers

1 gallon barbeque sauce

Directions

1. Wash and cut goat meat as directed into cubes. Soak overnight into in vinegar. Wash in clear Water. Combine spices Season goat. Grill meat until almost done. Cool.

Soak wooden skewers in water.

2. Cut vegetables and thread skewers with meat and vegetables. Complete grilling. Dip in barbeque sauce and serve.

Buffalo Chicken Wings

Number of servings-50; size of servings: 1/2 pound

Amount   Ingredients

25 pounds chicken wings, separated

1 gallon Buffalo chicken sauce

Directions

1. Clean chicken wings. Grill until done.
2. Place in large pans.
3. Add buffalo sauce, Cover and heat up. Serve.

Fried Drumsticks

Number of servings: 50; Size of servings: 2 per person

Amount Ingredients

12 pounds Drumsticks

1 cup garlic powder

1 cup black pepper

5 pounds self-rising flour

2 gallons corn oil

Directions

1. Wash and clean drum sticks. Season with garlic powder and pepper.
2. Dredge in flour; heat oil and deep fry drumsticks until

golden brown.
3. Serve hot.

Extra Hot Wings Sauce

Number of servings 50; size of servings 3 per person

Amount   Ingredients

20 pounds chicken wings

3 (6 ounces) bottles hot wings

5 pounds flour, all purpose

1/4 cup ground red pepper

5 -one gallon — sized plastic bags

6 large eggs

2 gallons peanut oil

Directions

1. Clean and wash chicken wings and place in plastic bags.
2. Pour hot sauce on wings for desired flavor or heat. Shake to coat chicken entirely. Close Bags and marinate for 2 hours.
3. Beat eggs in a medium-sized bowl.
4. Pour flour in separate Ziploc container; add cayenne pepper.
5. Coat wings in beaten eggs and the place each wing in flour mixture. Dust off. Place in the Refrigerate for 15 minutes; so flour will stick to chicken.
6. Preheat deep fryer to 370 degrees Fahrenheit
7. Deep fry wings until golden brown. Serve.

Spicy Fried Chicken Gizzards

Number of servings: 50; size of servings 1/2 pound

Amount Ingredients

50 pounds chicken gizzards

10 pounds self rising flour

2 cups black pepper

3 gallons peanut oil

Directions

1. Wash and dry chicken gizzards; Set aside. In a large plastic bag stir together, 1/5 of flour and And pepper; Dredge chicken gizzards in seasoned flour; dust off and deep fry in hot peanut oil. Drain.
2. Continue this process until all gizzards are cooked.
3. Serve on paper plates.

Popcorn Chicken

Number of servings-50; Size of servings- 5 pieces

Amount Ingredients

25 pounds chicken breast; cut into 1 inch portions

2 cups seasoning salt

5 gallons buttermilk

5 pounds self-rising flour

5 gallons peanut oil

Directions

1. Wash and cut up chicken breast. Season with scasoning salt.

2. Dip chicken in flour .Then dip in buttermilk. Then dip in flour again.
3. Deep fat fry in peanut oil. Drain. Serve.

Buffalo Chicken Wings

Number of servings 50; size of servings 4 wings

Amount   Ingredients

40 pounds chicken wing drummettes

5 pounds butter, melted

2 cups seasoning salt

10 cups hot sauce

Directions

1. Preheat oven to 350 degrees.
2. Wash and separate wings. Place wings into 10 large pans.
3. Season with seasoning salt. Pour butter over wings; bake for 30 minutes. Stir.
4. Evenly distribute hot sauce on wings. Bake until done. Serve on plastic plates.

Fried Chicken Necks

Number of servings 50; Size of servings -4 necks

Amount Ingredients

25 pounds chicken necks

21/2 cups seasoning salt

1/4 cup black pepper

4 pounds self-rising flour

5 gallons, peanut oil

1 quart hot sauce

Directions

1. Clean and wash chicken necks. Set aside. Add seasoning to flour.
2. Coat necks in flour.
3. Fry in hot peanut oil until golden brown. Drain. Serve with hot sauce.
4. Serve 4 per person.

Jerk Chicken

Number of servings-50; size of servings 2 drumsticks

Amount   Ingredients

100 chicken legs

5 pounds green onions

5 pounds yellow onions, chopped

2 pounds scotch bonnet peppers

2 tablespoons ground allspice

1/2 cup dried thyme

1/2 cup cayenne pepper

1/4 cup black pepper

1/2 cup sage

1/4 cup nutmeg

1/2 cup ground ginger

1/2 cup cinnamon

1/4 cup garlic powder

1 cup salt

4 cups olive oil

2 cups soy sauce

1 quart white vinegar

1/2 gallon orange juice

1/2 gallon molasses

Directions

1. Wash and clean chicken legs; set aside.
2. In a large container, mix together all seasonings, olive oil Soy sauce, white vinegar, orange juice and molasses. Stir well; add green onions and yellow onions
3. Divide into 5 portions and place into 5 large freezer bags. Coat the chicken well with jerk seasonings, seal and refrigerate overnight.
4. Remove chicken from marinade and boil marinade for 10 minutes. Cool and use marinade For basting sauce.
5. Grill chicken. Grill for one hour or until done.

Xtra Hot wings

Number of servings - 50; Size of servings-4.

Amount   Ingredients

20 pounds chicken wing drummettes

3 cups seasoning salt

1 cup cayenne (red) pepper

1 gallon extra red hot sauce

Directions

1. Clean grill. Wash wings. Dry wings. Put wings into two large deep aluminum pans; Season with seasoning salt and red pepper. Place on grill. Coat with extra hot sauce. Stir. Heat on grill for ten minutes before serving.
2. Serve four drummettes per person.

Teriyaki Chicken on Skewers

50 servings —2 skewers each

Amount	Ingredients
25 pounds	Boneless chicken breasts cut into 3 inch strips
4 gallons	Italian Salad Dressing
4 cups	Black Pepper, coarsely, grounded
4 cups	garlic salt
2 gallons	Teriyaki Sauce
100	wooden skewers
100	6-inch plastic plates

Directions

1. Wash chicken and cut into strips.
2. In three large containers, evenly divide chicken and pour 1 gallon each of Italian Dressing and stir. Cover and marinate in refrigerator oven night.
3. Combine black pepper and garlic salt. Save for later.
4. Soak wooden skewers in water thoroughly. Wash chicken. Season with black Pepper and garlic mix.
5. Grill chicken until done. Heat teriyaki sauce and add to chicken on plates.

Lemon Pepper Wings

6. Serve hot.

Lemon Pepper Wings

50—4 piece servings

Amount Ingredients

25 pounds chicken wings, separated into 3 parts

2-1 pound cans Lemon Pepper

2 cups Salt

1 pound can Onion flakes

1 pound can garlic powder

5 pounds Rice Flour

5 gallons Peanut Oil

Directions

1. Wash wings and separate into 4 parts. Pat dry.
2. Mix together lemon pepper, salt, onion flakes and garlic powder.
3. Season wings. Dredge in Rice Flour. Shake off excess flour.
4. Deep fry in peanut oil. Drain.
5. Serve hot

Nuts and others

Boiled Hot Spicy Peanuts

Number of servings-50 servings; Size of servings-i cup

Amount   Ingredients

25 pounds raw peanuts (Goober Peanuts in the shell)

4 cups cayenne pepper

4 cups salt

Water to cover

Directions

1. In two large pots, divide equally clean raw peanuts in the shell in the pots. Fill with water.
2. Add 2 cups cayenne pepper and 2 cups salt to each pot. Stir. Bring to a boil. Then reduce Heat. Cook covered for 45 minutes.

Roasted Goobers (Prepare ahead)

Number Of Servings: 50-8 Ounce Small Bags

Amount   Ingredients

25 Pounds Large Peanuts, Picked And Cleaned

4 Cups Salt

Water To Cover

Directions

1. Divide Peanuts Up Into 4 Large Pots. Cover with

water.
2. Stir in one cup of salt per pot.
3. Bring to a boil and then simmer for thirty minutes.
4. Drain and let dry for overnight.
5. Roast in the oven and bag up.
6. Serve

Onion Blossoms

Number Of Servings 50-1 Serving Per Person

Amount   Ingredients

50 Vidalia Onions, Peeled And Cut Into Blossoms

5 Pounds Pancake Mix

1 Cup Garlic Salt

1 Cup Seasoning Salt

2 Gallons Milk

1 Cup Sugar

5 Gallons Peanut Oil

1 Gallon Ranch Dressing Use 1/4 Cup Servings For Dipping Sauce

Directions

1. Prepare Onions As Directed. Wash And Dry. Set Aside.
2. In A Large Container, Mix Together Pancake Mix, Garlic Salt, Seasoning Salt, Milk And Sugar.
3. Heat Oil To 350 Degrees.
4. Dip Onions Individually In Pancake Batter.
5. Fry In Peanut Oil Until Golden Brown.
6. Serve Will Hot With Ranch Dressing For Dipping Sauce.

Souse Meat

50 servings — 1 slice

Amount   Ingredients

2 Hog Heads

4 Pig's Ears

4 Pig's Feet

4 Pig's Tails

4 Large Yellow Onions, Chopped

2 Stalks Celery, Chopped

2 Large Bell Peppers

½ Cup   Salt

5 Tablespoons Red Pepper Flakes

10 Whole Cloves

20 Whole Black Pepper Corns

1 Gallon White Distilled Vinegar

4 Cups Pimento, Chopped Finely

2 Packages Plain Gelatin

Directions

1. IN TWO LARGE POTS DIVIDE MEAT, ONIONS, CELERY AND BELL PEPPER. Cover with water. Cover and bring to a boil. Then simmer. Cook until meat falls off bones, Cool and remove meat. Save broth and strain. Chop meat finely and discard bones.
2. Place meat, broth and remaining ingredients, except

pimento peppers and gelatin.
3. In a large pot and stir add 2 gallons of water. Cook for 40 minutes Stir constantly; do not burn.
4. Cool and add pimento and gelatin.
5. Pour up into 5 loaf pans. Let set in refrigerator until congealed.
6. Slice and serve.

Fish —Appetizers

She Crab Soup

Number of servings -50; size of servings_1/2 cup

Amount Ingredients

10 pounds crabs, picked and cleaned and then chopped.

1 cup butter

1 1/2 cups celery, chopped

3 cups yellow onions, chopped

3 cups carrots, chopped

1/4 cup seasoning salt

2 cups flour

4 gallons chicken broth

2 gallons milk

Directions

1. In a large container, clean and chop crab meat into pieces. Set aside.
2. In a large commercial skillet, add butter, sauté celery, onions and carrots Until soft. Add seasoning salt.
3. Add flour, stir well, gradually add in chicken broth, boil until thick; add in milk.
4. Bring to a boil continue to boil until thick.
5. Add crabmeat and simmer for 30 minutes. Serve.

Deep Fried Pig Skins

50- 1/4 Pound Servings

Amount Ingredients

100 Pounds Pork Skins, Fresh (Get From The Meat House)

10 Gallons Peanut Oil

4 cups salt

Paper towels

50 pint size zip lock bags

Directions

1. Cut skins in 3 inches long and one inch wide portions. Wash and Dry.
2. Heat up oil and fry small batches at a time. Skins should be puffy.
3. Season with salt after done; while hot. Drain on paper towels. Bag up.
4. Serve.

Conch Salad

Number of servings 50; size of serving -1/2 cup

Amount Ingredients

10 pounds Conch meat, finely chopped

2 cups jalepeno peppers, thinly sliced

10 cups tomatoes, diced

6 cups apple cider vinegar

1/2 cup salt

Directions

1. Pick and wash conch meat
2. In a large pot, boil conch meat for 5 minutes. Drain.
3. In a large bowl, mix together meat and remaining ingredients. Stir well. Chill for 2 hours.
4. Serve in bowls.

Old Fashioned Boiled Crabs

Number of serving -50; Size of servings- I per person

Amount   Ingredients

25 pounds Blue Dungness Crab Legs

2 pounds Old Bay Crab seasoning

5 pounds butter, melted

1 gallon cocktail sauce for dipping sauce

Directions

1. Clean Crags and divide into three large pots add water to cover and add seasonings.
2. Bring to a boil. Boil crab legs for 10 minutes. Serve with butter or cocktail sauce.

Grilled Gulf Shrimp Kabobs

Number of servings 50; size of servings 2 kabobs

50 pounds Gulf Port Shrimp

50 wooden skewers

2 cups garlic flakes

6 cups butter

1 cup salt

Directions

1. Clean and separate shrimp. Set aside. Soak wooden skewers in water. Thread Shrimp on skewers. Season with garlic flakes. Store on ice until ready to grill. Season with salt and brush with butter when grilling.
2. Serve hot.

Deep Fried Craw Fish

Number of servings 50; size of servings -6

Amounts   Ingredients

20 pounds crawfish (cleaned)

2 bags Old Bay Seasoning

4 pounds fish fry mix

5 quarts corn oil

Directions

1. Clean Crawfish. Wash and pat dry
2. Mix seasoning mix with fish fry mix and stir together. Coat crawfish well. Dust off.
3. Deep fry in hot corn oil. Serve hot on paper plates.

Popcorn Shrimp

Number of servings 50; size of serving- 6

Amount   Ingredients

25 pounds small shrimp, cleaned and deveined

15 pounds coating mix

1 cup garlic, minced

1 cup thyme leaves

1 cup salt

1 cup cayenne pepper

1 cup ground pepper

5 gallon peanut oil

Directions

1. Wash and clean shrimp; Set aside. Add all seasoning to shrimp coating mix. Stir well.
2. Coat shrimp in mixture. Dust off, place in gallon -size plastic bags, until ready to cook.
3. Keep cool until ready to cook.
4. Heat peanut oil in deep fat fryer to 375 degrees Fahrenheit.
5. Fry shrimp until golden brown. Serve hot.

Fried Turkey Legs

Number of servings 50; size of servings -1 per person

Amount   Ingredients

50 Turkey legs

Seasonings

1/2 cup onion powder

1 1/2 cups garlic powder

1 cup dried oregano leaves

1 cup sweet basil

1 cup dried thyme leaves

1 cup black pepper

1/2 cup cayenne pepper

2 gallons corn oil.

Directions

1. Clean turkey legs.
2. Mix seasonings. Season turkey legs. Heat corn oil. Fry turkey legs until done.
3. Serve.

Appetizers-Game

Barbeque Deer Meatballs

Number of servings 50; size of servings-4 per person

Amount   Ingredients

30 pounds deer meat, finely ground

5 pounds hamburger meat

1 pound sausage meat

1/2 cup seasoning salt

1/2 cup black pepper

2 cups yellow onions, minced

3 cups bread crumbs

3 gallons barbeque sauce

Directions

1. Preheat oven to 350 degrees. Mix together all ingredients except barbeque sauce. Roll into 1 inch balls. In large pans, bake for 30-40 minutes.
2. Drain, add barbeque sauce and cook in oven for 15 minutes.
3. Serve into bowls with tooth picks.

Fried Rabbit Or Squirrels

50 Servings - 1/4 Rabbit Or Squirrel - Each Serving

Amount   Ingredients

25 rabbits, skinned and cleaned (USE SAME FOR SQUIRRELS)

2 gallons apple cider vinegar

5 gallons water

4 cups   garlic salt

4 cups   black pepper

5 cups   seasoning salt

10 pounds self-rising flour

10 gallons Peanut Oil

4 LARGE LOAVES WHITE BREAD

3 LARGE BOTTLES TABSCO SAUCE

Directions

1. Wash rabbits thoroughly and cut into fourths.
2. Mix together vinegar and water, Pour over rabbits. Cover and marinate overnight. In a large bowl, combine garlic salt, black pepper and seasoning salt. Set Aside.
3. Drain throw away marinade and wipe meat dry.
4. Season meat. Dredge meat in flour.
5. Fry in hot oil until golden brown and done.
6. Serve on white bread with tabasco sauce

Fried Alligator Tails

Number of serving -50; Size of servings -2 pieces

Amount Ingredients

1003 "X 2" slices) Alligator tail

3 gallons apple cider vinegar

2 gallons water

3 cups salt

10 pounds yellow corn meal

2 pounds flour, self rising

3 cups black pepper

1 cup garlic salt

4 gallons corn oil for frying

Directions

1. Wash and prepare alligator tail as indicate. Place in three shallow pans and set aside.
2. Mix vinegar, water and salt. Pour into equal parts over alligator meat. Cover and let marinate for4 hours.
3. Take from soaking mixture and wash well. Discard marinade.
4. Refrigerate meat for one hour.
5. Mix together corn meal, flour, and seasonings. Stir well/ Roll each piece of meat into corn meal mixture until well-mixed.
6. Heat oil ad fry meat until golden brown. Serve hot on paper towel on paper plates.

Soups, Stews

Brunswick stew

50 servings -1/2 cup servings

2 hog heads, cleaned and washed

2 Chickens, cut-up

1-4 pound pork butt

3 pounds beef ribs

4 yellow onions cubed and divided

5 cups celery, chopped

1-1 pound can tomato sauce

1-1 pound tomato paste

2-1 pound cans creamed corn

2-1 pound cans green peas

3 Bottles Tabasco sauce

2-1 pound cans tomatoes, chopped

3 Tablespoons salt

2 tablespoons black pepper

1 gallon ketup

4 pounds potatoes diced

2 gallons water

Directions

1. in a large ten gallon sauce pot or large black pot place together hog heads, chicken, pork butt beef ribs, Y of the yellow onions and celery. Cover with water about four inches left over the top. Bring to a boil until done. Cool. Separate out all bones; chop meat and strain broth. 2, Discard bones and divide equally into pots. Divide all remaining equally between the two Pots and simmer for 11/2 hours until desired.
2. Serve over rice or with crackers

Kentucky Burgoos

Number of servings 50; size of servings -1 cup

Amount	Ingredients

6 frying chickens, cut up

1 pound pork roast

4 pounds beef short ribs

1 pound ham hocks

10 cups, red potatoes, diced

5 cups yellow onions, diced

5 cups carrots, sliced

2 cups bell peppers, diced

2(15 ounces can) whole kernel corn

2 cups okra, cut-up

2 cups lima beans, thawed

2 cups tomato puree

1 cup celery, diced

1 tablespoon salt

1 tablespoon black pepper

1 teaspoon crushed red pepper flakes

Directions

1. Wash and prepare chicken. Place all meat in a large stock pot and boil until tender.
2. Remove bones and add remaining ingredients. Cook covered until desired doneness.
3. Serve in 1 cup bowls.

Red Beansand Rice

Number of servings 30, Size of servings 4 cup beans over 1/2 cup rice

Amounts   Ingredients

15 cups pinto beans or kidney beans

Water to cover

6 cups yellow onions diced

3 bay leaves

1/4 cup garlic cloves, minced

2 tablespoons salt

2 cups crispy celery, chopped

2 cups green pepper, chopped

3 tablespoons seasoning salt

2 tablespoons cayenne pepper

4 pounds smoked sausage, chopped

25 cups cooked fluffy white rice

Directions

1. Soak beans in water to cover overnight. Drain. Add water to cover all ingredients, except sausage and rice. Cover.
2. Bring to a boil. Lower heat and cook until done.
3. Add smoked sausage and cook for 15 extra minutes. Serve over rice.

Boiled Collard Greens

50-1/2 Cup Servings

Amounts   Ingredients

6 Smoked Turkey Necks

6smoked Turkey Wings Cut Into 2 Inch Pieces

5 Cured Pig Tails, Cut Up

3 Gallons Water

12 Bunches Of Collard Greens, Picked, Washed, Cut-Up

3 Cups Shortening

1/2 Cup Red Pepper Flakes-Per Pot

1/3 Cup Salt—Per Pot

2 Tablespoons Sugar Per Pot

Directions

1. In Three Large Sauce Pots, Divide Meat And Boil In Water Until Tender.
2. Remove Bones From Meat And Return To Broth. Discard Bones.
3. Stir In Collard Greens In Each Pot- 3 Bunches Per

Pot.

4. Add Seasoning As Indicated. Bring to a boil for 5 minutes. Stirring constantly.
5. Medium boil for about 11/2 hours or until desired doneness.
6. Serve with corn patties or corn bread.

Low Country Boil

50=1 cup servings

Amount   Ingredients

4 Cups Old Bay Seasoning For Low Country Boil

5 Gallons Water

4 Pounds White Potatoes, Diced

10 Pounds Beef —Links, Sausages Cut Into 2 Inch Links

10 Pounds Crab Legs

5 Pounds Corn Cobbettes

10 Pounds Shrimp, Cleaned And Deveined

1 Cup Seasoning Salt

Directions

1. In A Large Black Pot About 10 Gallons, Add Old Bay Seasoning, Water And Potatoes. Cover And Boil Until Potatoes Are Almost Done.
2. Stir Well Gradually Add In Remaining Ingredients Except For Shrimp Ane) Seasoning Salt. Stir Well. CooK For Ten Minutes
3. Add Shrimp And Seasoning Salt And Cook Until Shrimp Turns Pink.
4. Cool Until Warm Enough To Serve

Cheddar Cheese Kabobs

Number of serving-SO; Size of serving -2 kabobs

Amounts   Ingredients

5 pounds Cheddar cheese, cubes,

Assorted flavors

5 pounds grape tomatoes, washed and cleaned

5 pounds Thompson seedless grapes

100 large cocktail tooth picks

Directions

1. Make kabobs by alternating cheeses, tomatoes and grapes.
2. Complete until 100 tooth picks are threaded.
3. Serve on hor's d'oeuvres.

APPETIZERS — VEGETABLES and FRUITS

Blackeyed Peas Caviar/Chips

Number of servings -50; size of servings 1/2 cup

Amount   Ingredients

1-(number 10 can) black eyed peas, drained

2 cups yellow onions, minced

4 cups green peppers, chopped

2 cups celery, minced

1 quart Italian dressing

5 large bags corn chips or preferred chips

Directions

1. In a colander drain black eyed peas. Place all ingredients except chips ,in a large bowl. Toss very well.
2. Chill for 5 hours. Serve with chips.

Baked Sweet Potatoes

Number of servings 50; size of servings -1 sweet potato per person

Amount   Ingredients

50 sweet potatoes

2 pounds butter, softened

Aluminum foil

Directions

1. Wash sweet potatoes, pierce potatoes with a fork to make holes. Wipe dry and rub with butter.
2. Wrap each potato individually with aluminum foil. Bake at 350 degrees Fahrenheit for One hour or grill for one hour or until done. Cool and serve.

Grilled Asparagus/Red Pepper Rings

Number of servings 50; size of servings 3 ounce portions

Amounts Ingredients

10 pounds asparagus, fresh stalks

5 pounds red bell peppers cut into rings

2 cups butter, melted

Directions

1. Wash and prepare asparagus and red peppers
2. Place on large baking sheet pans and spread with butter
3. Place on grill in pans and grill until desired doneness.

Hot Cheese Grits

50-1 Cup Servings

Amount   Ingredients

10 gallons Water, boiling

2 cups   salt

5 pounds Aunt Jemima -Quick cooking Grits

10 pounds Cheddar cheese, medium flavor, grated

Directions

1. Divide water into two 5 gallon saucepots, Bring to a boil add a cup salt to each saucepot. Divide grits and stir in equal amount of grits in each pot.
2. Cover and bring to a boil for about 5 minutes continue to stir. Then simmer until desired doneness. Stir in cheese. Serve hot,

Grilled Corn on the Cob

Number of servings -30; size of servings —one per person

Amount   Ingredients

50 count corn -on- the cob

3 cups butter

2 tablespoons salt

Aluminum foil

Directions

1. Place corn in a large bowl. Rub with butter. Wrap each ear with aluminum foil.
2. Grill corn. Keep corn on grill until ready to serve.

Guacamole Dip /Corn Chips

Number of servings -50; size of servings Y4 cup

Amounts   Ingredients

10 cups avocado, chopped

1/4 cup lemon juice

4 cups mayonnaise

2 cups sour cream

1 cup tomatoes, chopped

2 tablespoons salt

7 large bags tortilla chips
Directions

1. In food processer, process all ingredients except chips.
2. Refrigerate for 2 hours. Serve.

Fried Green Tomatoes

Number of serving 50; size of servings 4 slices per person

Amount   Ingredients

100 green tomatoes, washed

2 cups salt

1 cup black pepper

4 cups flour, all purpose

10 large eggs, beaten

10 cups yellow corn meal

2 gallons peanut oil

Directions

1. Wash and slice green tomatoes. Pat dry. Set aside. Add salt, black pepper and flour together. Set aside. Beat eggs in a bowl.
2. Coat tomatoes with flour mixture. Then eggs and then roll in corn meal. Fry to golden brown in peanut oil.

Marinated miniature Carrots/ Broccoli Flowerets, Red Radishes Melody

Number of servings 50; size of serving 1/4 cup per person

Amount Ingredients

10 pounds each miniature carrots, broccoli flowerets and red radishes

1 gallon Italian dressing

Directions

1. Wash carrots, broccoli and radishes. Cut tops and bottoms from radishes.
2. Put equal parts of vegetables into two large containers. Pour Italian dressing on vegetables.
3. Cover and refrigerate. Marinate for 4 hours stirring every 30 minutes. Serve.

Salsa /Chips

Number of servings 50; size of serving % cups

Amount   Ingredients

10 pounds Roma tomatoes, chopped

1/4 pound jalepeno peppers, minced

2 garlic bulbs, minced

1 cup lime juice

2 cups white onions minced

2 cups green peppers, minced

Chips

Directions

1. Prepare vegetables as directed. Add garlic, lime juice, onions and green peppers.
2. Stir well. Refrigerate 4 hours before serving. Serve with chips.

Spicy Cherry Tomatoes

Number of servings 50; size of serving -1/2 cup

Amount   Ingredients

8 gallons red cherry tomatoes

1 quart white onions, minced

1 quart celery, minced

2 cups seasoning salt

1 cup garlic salt

1 cup cayenne pepper

1 1/2 gallon Italian Dressing

Directions

1. Wash tomatoes and cut into halves. In a large container add onions celery and stir well.
2. Add remaining seasonings and toss well. Cover Refrigerate for 1 hour and add dressing and serve.

Appetizers - Mixed Fruit Cup

Number of servings 50; size of servings -1/2 cup per person

Amount   Ingredients

25 cups Pineapples, fresh, cut into chunks

9 cups delicious apples, cut into slices

4 cups maraschino cherries

5 cups peaches, diced

Directions

1. Prepare pineapples as directed as indicated.
2. In large containers, add all fruits and stir.
3. Place in 1/2 cup Styrofoam cups and cover with a lid. Refrigerate until serving.

Fresh Seedless Grape Kabobs

Amount   Ingredients

10 pounds large black seedless grapes

5 pounds Fresh pineapple cut into chunks

5 Pounds Red Seedless Grapes

10 pounds Strawberries

6 large bags Marshmallows,

50 wooden skewers, soaked in water

Directions

1. Wash fruit and assemble.
2. Begin with grapes and end with grapes.

Marinated Broccoli Spears

50 -1/2 Cup Broccoli Spears Florets

Amount   Ingredients

15 Pounds Fresh Broccoli Spears, Cut Into 2 Inch Size Florets

7 Cups Italian Dressing

5 Tablespoons Red Pepper Flakes

1 Cup Sugar

Directions

1. Wash And Prepare Broccoli Spears As Directed. Set Aside And Chill In Refrigerator/
2. Combine Italian Dressing, Red Pepper Flakes And Sugar. Stir Well.
3. 5 Mnutes Before Serving, Pour Over Broccoli Florets. Serve In 1/2 Cup Bowls.

Hush Puppies

50 Servings - 2 Per Person

Amount   Ingredients

5 Pounds Yellow Corn Meal Mix

1 Pound Minced Yellow Onions

1 Pound Green Onions Chooped

1 1/2 Quarts Of Water

5 Gallons Peanut Oil, For Frying

Paper Towels

Directions

1. In a large bowl, mix together yellow corn meal, onions and water, should be stiff dough.
2. Make into 2 inches long balls.
3. Heat oil and fry hush puppies until golden brown. Drain. Serve.

Grilled Cantaloupe

50—2 slices per person

Amount

5 large cantaloupes, sliced into 10 slices

2 tablespoons cinnamon

4 cups sugar

Aluminum foil

50 Plastic plates

Directions

1. Peel and seed cantaloupes
2. Mix sugar with cinnamon.
3. Spray aluminum foil with pam spray. Line 10 cantaloupe slices per sheet.
4. Sprinkle with cinnamon mixture and grille to desired doneness
5. Serve on plastic plates.

ALBANY STATE UNIVERSITY

ALBANY, GEORGIA

MOTTO: Potential, Realized.

HISTORY: Founded in 1903 (Public University-Urban-204 Acres)

ENROLLMENT: 4,176

DEGREES GRANTED: Undergraduate, graduate, liberal arts and professional degrees

NICKNAME/MASCOT: Golden Rams

SCHOOL COLORS: Royal Blue and Yellow Gold

NAME OF MARCHING BAND: The Marching Rams Show Band

NAME OF STADIUM: Albany Municipal Coliseum Stadium

SPORTS: Basketball, Cross-Country, Football, Outdoor Track, Softball, Tennis, Volleyball

CLASSIC BOWL GAMES: FOUNTAIN CITY CLASSIC- Albany State University vs Fort Valley State University @Columbus, GA

2) MUSIC CITY CLASSIC —Savannah State University vs Albany State University @

Macon, GA

BENEDICT COLLEGE

COLUMBIA, SOUTH CAROLINA

MOTTO: A Power for Good in Society.

HISTORY: Founded in 1870 (Private, Baptist Churc-110 acres)

ENROLLMENT: 2500+

DEGREES GRANTED: Bachelor degrees -29 undergraduate degrees from 12 departments

NICKNAME/MASCOT: BC Tigers

SCHOOL COLORS: Purple and Gold

NAME OF STADIUM: Charles W. Johnson Stadium

NAME OF MARCHING BAND: Marching Band of Distinction

SPORTS: Basketball, football, volleyball, baseball, softball, track and field, cross country, golf, soccer, tennis, volleyball

CLASSIC BOWL GAMES: 1) LABOR DAY CLASSIC — Benedict College vs Tuskegee University @ Columbia, South Carolina

2) CAPITAL CITY PALMETTO CLASSIC —South Carolina State University Vs Benedict @ Columbia, South Carolina

3) SAVANNAH RIVER AREA CLASSIC — Clark-Atlanta vs Benedict College @Augusta, Georgia

CLARK-ATLANTA UNIVERSITY

ATLANTA, GEORGIA

MOTTO: "I'll Find a way or Make one" (Atlanta University) and "Culture for Service"(Clark College)

HISTORY: Founded 1988 (Uniting of Clark College 1865 and Atlanta University, Private 126 acres)

(Atlanta University established under United Methodist Church in 1869- Atlanta University -The nation's oldest HBCU granting graduate degrees). (Private University-Urban Campus)

ENROLLMENT: 5,000

DEGREES GRANTED: Undergraduate, graduate, specialists and doctoral and professional degrees.

SCHOOL COLORS: Red, Black and Gray.

NICKNAME/MASCOT: Black Panther

NAME OF STADIUM: PANTHERS STADIUN

NAME OF MARCHING BAND: Mighty Marching Panther Band

SPORTS: Baseball, Basketball, Cross-Country, Football, Outdoor Track, Soccer, Softball, Tennis, Volleyball

CLASSIC BOWL GAMES: 1) GOLD COAST CLASSIC — Clark-Atlanta vs Fort Valley State University @Brunswick, GA

2) SAVANNAH RIVER AREA CLASSIC-Clark-Atlanta vs Benedict College @Augusta, GA

FORT VALLEY STATE UNIVERSITY

Fort Valley, Georgia

MOTTO: 'THE FORT VALLEY STATE UNIVERSITY ISA LIGHT FOR YOUR PATH"

HISTORY: Founded 1895 (Public —Land —Grant University-Rural 1365 acres)

(Home of Flag Allegedly draped President Abraham Lincoln Coffin)

ENROLLMENT: 4,106

DEGREES GRANTED: Bachelor's degrees in 50 programs, masters degrees arid specialist degrees.

SCHOOL COLORS: Royal Blue and Gold

NICKNAME/MASCOT: Wildcats/Lady Wildcats

NAME OF MARCHING BAND: Marching Blue Machine

NAME OF STADIUM: Wildcat Stadium

SPORTS: Basketball, Outdoor Track, Football, Volleyball

CLASSIC BOWL GAMES: 1) FOUNTAIN CITY CLASSIC —Fort Valley State University vs Albany State University @ Columbus, Georgia)

2) STAN LOMAX GOLD COAST CLASSIC —Fort Valley State University vs Clarke Atlanta, @Bruriswick, GA

LANE UNIVERSITY

JACKSON, TENNESSEE

MOTTO: Esse Non Viden

HISTORY: Founded 1882 (Established by Christian Methodist Episcopal Church-Private University — Urban campus- 25 acres Liberal arts)

ENROLLMENT: 2500 students

DEGREES GRANTED: Bachelor's degrees in three major areas : 1) Business and Social and Behavioral Sciences, 2) Liberal Studies and Education 3) Natural and Physical Sciences

NICKNAME/MASCOT: Dragons

SCHOOL COLORS: Cardinal Red and Royal Blue

NAME OF STADIUM: Rothrock Stadium

SPORTS: Baseball, Basketball, Cross-country, Football, Tennis, Softball, Volleyball, Track and field

NAME OF MARCHING BAND: Lane College Marching Band

CLASSIC BOWL GAMES: MEMPHIS BLUES CLASSIC

1) Virginia Union University vs Lane College © Memphis, TN

MILES COLLEGE

Fairfield, Ala

HISTORY: Founded 1898 (Established by Christian Methodist Episcopal Church- Private Liberal Arts -76 acres)

ENROLLMENT: 1738

DEGREES GRANTED: 25 Baccalaureate degrees and a degree in law.

SCHOOL COLORS: Purple and Gold

NICKNAME/MASCOT: Golden Bears

NAME OF MARCHING BAND: Miles Purple Marching Band

NAME OF STADIUM: Alumni Stadium (Albert J. Sloan)

SPORTS: Baseball, Basketball, Cross-Country Track, Track and Field, Football, Softball, Volleyball,

CLASSIC BOWL GAMES: 1) A. G. GASTON LABOR DAY CLASSIC —Tuskegee University vs Miles College @ Legion Field Birmingham, AL

2) STEEL CITY CLASSIC — Stillman University vs Miles College @Legion Field

Birmingham, Al.

MOREHOUSE COLLEGE

ATLANTA, GEORGIA

MOTTO: "Et Facta Est Lux "(And there was Light)

HISTORY: Founded in 1867 (Founded in 1787 in Augusta Baptist Church the oldest independent African-American Church in USA-later Morehouse College moved to Atlanta-Private all-Male- Private-Urban Campus)

ENROLLMENT: 2900

DEGREES GRANTED: Baccalaureate degrees

SCHOOL COLORS: Maroon and white

NICKNAME/MASCOT: Maroon Tigers

NAME OF MARCHING BAND: Morehouse College Maroon Marching Band

NAME OF STADIUM: B.T. Harvey Stadium

SPORTS: Basketball, Football, baseball, cross-country, tennis, track and field, golf

CLASSIC BOWL GAMES: 1) TUSKEGEE-MOREHOUSE CLASSIC —Morehouse University vs Tuskegee University @ McClung Stadium — Columbus, GA

KENTUCKY STATE UNIVERSITY

Frankfort, Kentucky

MOTTO: Enter to Learn; Exit to Serve

HISTORY: Founded 1886 (Public University—Land Grant -511 acres)

ENROLLMENT: 2,341

DEGREES GRANTED: Baccalaureate degrees

SCHOOL COLORS: Green and Gold

NICKNAME/MASCOT: Thorobreds

NAME OF MARCHING BAND: Thoroughbreds Express

NAME OF STADIUM: Alumni Stadium

SPORTS: Baseball, Basketball, Cross Country, Football, Golf, Indoor Track, Outdoor Track, Softball, Tennis, Volleyball

CLASSIC BOWL GAMES: 1) HERTIAGE CLASSIC — Kentucky State University vs Allen University @ Dunbar Stadium, Lexington, Kentucky

2) ST.LOUIS GATEWAY CLASSOC — Kentucky State University vs. Arkansas Pine

Bluff University @ St. Louis, MO

STILLMAN COLLEGE

TUSCALOOSA, ALABAMA

HISTORY: Founded in 1876 (Private, HBCU)

ENROLLMENT: 1500

DEGREES GRANTED: Baccalaureate

SCHOOL COLORS: Navy Blue and Vegas Gold

NICKNAME'MASCOT: Tigers/Lady Tigers

NAME OF MARCHING BAND: Blue Pride Marching Band

NAME OF STADIUM: Stillman Stadium

SPORTS: Baseball, Basketball, Cross-Country, Football, Softball, Tennis, volleyball

TUSKEGEE UNIVERSITY

TUSKEGEE, ALABAMA

MOTTO: Scientia Principatus Opera - Science Participate Deeds (Knowledge, Nation, Deeds)

HISTORY: Founded July 4, 1881 (Booker T. Washington First President, Private-Land-Grant — Rural 5000 acres)

ENROLLMENT: 2700

DEGREES GRANTED: 34 bachelor degree programs, 12 masters degree programs, a degree in architecture, 2 doctoral degree programs, doctor of veterinary medicine, master's and doctoral degrees in engineering.

SCHOOL COLORS: Crimson and Old Gold

NICKNAME/MASCOT: Golden Tigers

NAME OF MARCHING BAND: Marching Crimson Piper Band

NAME OF STADIUM: Abbot Memorial Alumni Stadium

SPORTS: Baseball, Basketball, Cross-Country, Football, Outdoor Track, Softball, Tennis, Volleyball

CLASSIC BOWL GAMES: 1) AG. GASTON LABOR DAY CLASSIC — Tuskegee University vs Miles College @ Legion Field, Birmingham, Ala.

2) LABOR DAY CLASSIC — Benedict College vs. Tuskegee University @ Columbia, South Carolina

3) RIVERFRONT CLASSIC — Hampton vs Tuskegee @Cleveland Brown Stadium Cleveland, Ohio (Sponsored by Proctor and Gamble Corporation)

4) TUSKEGEE-MOREHOUSE CLASSIC —Morehouse University vs Tuskegee University @McClung Stadium- Columbus, GA

5) TURKEY DAY CLASSIC - Tuskegee University vs. Alabama State Univ At Cramton Bowl, Montgomery, Al

ENTREES/SWAC

SOUTHWESTERN ATHLETIC CONFERENCE
SWAC
1920

ALABAMA A&M UNIVERSITY - BULLDOGS - HUNTSVILLE, ALABAMA

ALABAMA STATE UNIVERSITY-HORNETS-MONTGOMERY, ALABAMA

ALCORN STATE UNIVERSITY - BRAVES - ALCORN STATE, MISSISSIPPI

GRAMBLING STATE UNIVERSITY - TIGERS - GRAMBLING, LOUISIANA

JACKSON STATE UNIVERSITY - TIGERS - JACKSON, MS

MISSISSIPPI VALLEY STATE UNIVERSITY - ITTA BENA, MISSISSIPPI, DELTA DEVILS/DEVILETTES

PRAIRIE VIEW A&M UNIVERSITY - PRAIRIE, TEXAS - PANTHERS

SOUTHERN UNIVERSITY-JAGUARS - BATON ROUGE, LA

TEXAS SOUTHERN UNIVERSITY TIGERS - HOUSTON, TEXAS

UNIVERSITY OF ARKANSAS AT PINE BLUFF - PINE BLUFF, ARK - GOLDEN LIONS

Beef

Barbeque Beef Ribs

(Number of servings-50; size of servings —2 ribs)

Ingredients

20 pounds of beef ribs

1 gallon Italian dressing

3 cups onions finely chopped

5 tablespoons garlic salt

1/2 cups black pepper

2 gallons favorite barbeque sauce

Directions

1. Wash and clean ribs. Place in large foil pans.
2. In a large bowl combine Italian dressing, onions, garlic salt and black pepper.
3. Pour over meat and marinate overnight. Discard marinade.
4. Prepare grill and grill ribs until tender,
5. Add barbeque sauce to ribs in pan and continue to grill.
6. Serve.

Smoked Baron of Beef

(number of servings -50, size of servings 1/2 pound sliced)

Ingredients

30 pounds special cut baron of beef (special cut by butcher)

Rub mix:

4 cups seasoning salt

1 cup garlic salt

1 cup Kosher salt

1 gallon Italian dressing

1/2 gallon teriyaki sauce

50 Wheat buns

Directions

1. Clean and wash beef. Rub dry. Prepare Smoker
2. In a large bowl, mix together seasoning salt, garlic salt and Kosher salt . Mix well.
3. Mix together Italian dressing and teriyaki sauce. Stir in salt mix.
4. Evenly rub mixture on meat.
5. Place meat on smoker and cook to an internal temperature of 165 degrees Fahrenheit ;about 14-16 hours.
6. Let rest for 30 minutes. Slice and serve on buns.

Barbeque Beef Brisket

(Number of servings-50, size of servings -1 sandwich)

Ingredients

3-10 pound beef briskets

Rub:

1/2 cup seasoning salt

1/4 cup black pepper

1/4 cup cayenne pepper

2 tablespoons salt

1/3 cup chili pepper

2 tablespoons cumin

1 gallon commercial barbeque sauce

50 onion -flavored hoagie buns

Directions

1. Wash briskets, take off excess fat or gristle. Set aside.
2. In a large bowl, add together all seasonings. Rub over meat.
3. Cover and refrigerate meat for 6 hours before grilling.
4. Prepare grill and grill meat slowly for 8 hours. Slice thinly and place into large pans
5. Spread barbeque sauce over meat. Cover and bake in oven at 350 degrees Fahrenheit until done.
6. Serve on buns wrapped individually.

TAILGATING SPAGHETTI

50—1 cup servings

Amount	Ingredients
1 Cup	Vegetable oil
4 cups	onions, diced
4 cups	Celery, diced
1/2 cup	Garlic, minced
4 cups	Bell pepper, diced
10 pounds	Ground beef

1 gallon can Tomato sauce

2 cups Tomato paste

1 quart Ketchup

1 quart Spaghetti Sauce

11/2 quarts Water

Salt and pepper to taste

4 packages Spaghetti Noodles, prepare according to directions

Directions

1. In a 10 quart stockpot, heat oil and cook all vegetable until tender.
2. Gradually add in meat, stir constantly. Cook until all red has let meat.
3. Stir in remaining ingredients. Cook for 30 minutes. Season with salt and pepper to taste.
4. Serve over previously cook spaghetti noodles.

Beef Chili

(Number of servings 50;size of servings- one bowl)

Ingredients

15 pounds of lean hamburger meat

4 yellow onions, finely chopped

1 cup chili powder 1/2 cup cumin

1 tablespoon paprika

2 cups green peppers diced

1(number 10 can) tomato sauce

1/2 gallon water

2- (number 10 cans) whole tomatoes, diced

Directions

1. In a large cooker, brown beef and drain. Stir in onions. Add spices. Cover for 30 minutes.
2. Add green peppers and tomato sauce. Continue to stir.
3. Add 1/2 gallon of water. Stir in tomatoes and continue to simmer for 30 minutes.
4. Serve over rice or with tortilla chips.

Chipped Barbeque Beef

(Number of servings 50; size of servings-5 ounces on bun)

Ingredients

2- 20 pounds beef sirloin wholesale cuts

Rub:

1/4 cup seasoning salt

2 tablespoons cayenne pepper

3 tablespoons black pepper

11/2 teaspoons chili pepper

2 tablespoons soul seasoning

Sauce:

1 quart molasses

1 pint apple cider vinegar

2 cups yellow mustard

1 1/2 cups yellow onions, chopped

2 cups brown sugar

2 gallons commercial barbeque sauce

Directions

1. Wash beef and pat dry. Set aside. Prepare grill.
2. Mix together ingredients for rub.
3. Take mixture and rub on beef.
4. Grill beef slowly until tender.
5. While beef is cooking, prepare sauce on grill cook for 30 minutes, stirring constantly and Then remove from heat.
6. When meat is done. Chip with knife into bite size pieces and place in large aluminum pans.
7. Pour barbeque sauce over meat and stir the mixture well. Cover with foil and continue to cook on grill or in oven until desired doneness. Serve on buns.

Grilled Beef Kabobs

(Number of servings-SO; size of servings one kabob)

Ingredients

25 pounds Angus boneless sirloin, cut into 2 squares

1 gallon apple juice

2 gallons Italian salad dressing

2 cups Kosher salt

10 pounds red and green bell pepper, cut into 1" inch squares

5 pounds red onions, cut into 1" inch squares

50 wooden kabob sticks

1 gallon apple juice

Directions

1. Cut beef into portions. Wash and place in pans with marinade of apple juice, Italian dressing and salt.
2. Marinate overnight.
3. Soak 50 wooden sticks in water for one hour.
4. Thread each wooden stick with beef, peppers and onions.
5. Grill until done. Baste with apple juice during grilling.
6. Serve one kabob per person

Grilled Beef Sausage

(Number of servings-50; size of servings 1 sausage dog)

50 pounds of beef sausage, preferred -brand

10 pounds white onions, sliced

10 pounds green peppers, sliced

50 wheat rolls

Directions

1. Wash sausages and divide into equal portions.
2. Prepare onions and green peppers.
3. Prepare grill and grill sausages and vegetables until done.
4. Serve on buns with condiments.

Grilled Beef Rolled Roast

(Number of servings-50; size of servings-1/2 pound)

Amounts   Ingredients

6-5 pounds boneless rolled prime ribs roast

3 cups worchestershire sauce

1 gallon commercial barbeque sauce

50 whole wheat buns

Directions

1. Prepare cuts of meat. Please in large pans. Set aside.
2. In a large bowl, combine worchestershire sauce and Italian dressing. Mix well. Pour over meat.
3. Cover meat with aluminum foil, Refrigerate and marinate overnight.
4. Next day discard marinade and pat meat dry. Place on grill in pans. Grill until desired doneness.
5. Carve and serve on buns with barbeque sauce.

Barbeque Chipped Beef

(Number of servings-50, size of servings ;1/4 pound on hamburger bun)

Ingredients

20 pounds boneless side beef

2 cups minced onions

1 cup brown sugar

1/4 cup chili powder

1 tablespoon ground cinnamon

1 tablespoon ground cumin

3 cups apple cider vinegar

2 gallons barbeque sauce

50 hamburger buns

Directions

1. Wash and prepare beef. Set aside.
2. In a bowl, stir together the next six ingredients.

3. Rub generously on meat. Place on grill and grill over medium heat.
4. When meat is almost done, place in aluminum pans and gradually add one half of barbeque sauce.
5. Remove from grill; chip. Then add remaining barbeque sauce. Continue to grill for 30 minutes Or until desired doneness. Serve on buns.

Grilled Filet Mignons

50 filet mignon steaks individually wrapped in bacon

10 pounds red onions, sliced

1 quart olive oil

50 buns

Directions

1. Prepare grill and coat with cooking spray.
2. Grill meat 5 minutes on both sides and then add onions on grill. Stir well.
3. Serve on a bun on a paper plate

Grilled Philly Cheese Steak Sandwich

(Number of servings-50; size of servings -1 sandwich)

Ingredients

25 pounds thinly sliced roast beef

10 pounds sliced onions

10 pounds sliced green peppers

1/2 cup seasoning salt

50 slices American Cheese

50 hoagie buns

Directions

1. Grilled beef until done. Grill vegetables and season with seasoning salt. Make individual sandwiches and place cheese on top of hoagie buns.
2. Serve on paper plate.

Ground Beef Chili

(Number of Servings -50; Size of servings-1 cup)

Ingredients

5 large yellow onions

10 pounds Ground Sirloin

1 cup chili powder

1 cup seasoning salt

2 tablespoons black pepper

5 (10.75-ounce) can Tomato Soup

5 (14.5 —ounce) cans Diced Tomatoes with Sweet Onions (undrained)

5 (10 ounces) cans Rotel Milder Diced Tomatoes and Green Chilies (undrained)

5 (16 ounces) cans Bush's Best Chili Beans (undrained)

3 (15 —ounce) cans Bush's Best Black Beans (drained)

Directions

1. Remove ends and peels from onions, chop onions coarsely and divide in half. Preheat large Sauce pot at medium heat 2-3 minutes. Place beef, chili powder,

seasoning salt, pepper And one half of the onion in sauce pot. Cook :10 minutes, stirring to crumble meat, or until meat is brown and no pink remains.

2. Stir in remaining ingredients, including remaining one-half onions. Bring to a boil, stirring often.
3. Reduce heat to low, cook 30 minutes, stirring occasionally, to blend flavors. Serve.

Grilled Hamburgers

(Number of servings-50; size of serving - one burger)

Ingredients

15 pounds ground chuck

2 pounds yellow onions minced

1 pound celery minced

1 pound green pepper, minced

1 pound cracker crumbs

1 dozen eggs, whipped

2 tablespoons salt

3 tablespoons black pepper

50 Hamburger buns

Directions

1. In a large bowl combine all ingredients. Stir very well.
2. Make out into 50 or more 4- inch in diameter meat patties.
3. Cover and refrigerate patties for 4 hours.
4. Grill patties on both sides until done.
5. Serve with condiments on buns.

Grilled New York Strips

(Number of servings -50; size of serving; 1 steak sandwich)

Ingredients

50 New York Strips, cut into 1 —inch thick strips

1/2 cup seasoning salt

1/4 cup cracked black pepper

50 whole wheat steak buns

Directions

1. Wash and dry steaks. Season.
2. Prepare grill and grill steaks on both sides.
3. Serve on buns.

Grilled Porterhouse Steak

(Number of servings- 50; size of servings — one steak per person)

Ingredients

50 Porterhouse steaks, special cut from butcher

1/2 cup seasoning salt

1/2 cup garlic salt

50 whole wheat steak buns

Directions:

1. Wash and dry steaks. Set aside.
2. Mix together seasoning salt and garlic salt.
3. Sprinkle over meat.
4. Prepare grill and grill.
5. Serve on bun.

Grilled Sirloin Steaks

50 -1/2 pound sirloin steaks

1/2 gallon olive oil

1 gallon apple juice

1 gallon peach nectar

1/2 cup black pepper

1/2 cup salt

1/2 cup seasoning salt

Directions

1. Wash and prepare steaks; set aside.
2. Combine olive oil, apple juice and peach nectar.
3. Pour over steak; cover and marinate overnight.
4. Discard marinade and prepare grill.
5. Grill on both sides until done.
6. Serve on bun.

Memphis Barbeque Beef Ribs

(Number of servings 50; size of servings- one rib sandwich)

Ingredients

25 pounds beef ribs —cut into 2 inch long pieces

4 liters coca cola

5 garlic cloves, minced

6 cups teriyaki sauce

1 cup black pepper

2 gallons commercial barbeque sauce

1 gallon ketchup

2 cups brown sugar

50 steak buns

Directions

1. Clean and wash beef ribs. In a large pan, combine the next four ingredients.
2. Pour over steaks for two hours turn and marinate for one hours
3. Discard marinade and prepare grill.
4. Grill on both sides until desired doneness.
5. Add together commercial barbeque sauce, ketchup and brown sugar. Stir. Bring to a boil
6. Cover ribs with sauce.

Grilled Polish Sausages

(Number of servings -50; Size of serving; 1 link sandwich)

Ingredients

25 pounds Polish sausages — 2 links per person

Directions

1. Prepare sausages
2. Spray grill with olive oil.
3. Grill until done.
4. Serve on bun.

Pork

Baby Back Ribs

(Number of servings 50; Size of servings- 1 sandwich)

Ingredients

10 pounds baby back ribs

Marinade

8 cloves garlic, minced

1 quart molasses

5 cups apple cider vinegar

2 cups vegetable oil

Rub

1 cup Kosher salt

1 cup cracked black pepper

1 pound light brown sugar

1 cup cumin

Barbeque sauce

2 cups dark brown sugar

1 quart ketchup

10 ounces chili sauce

2 yellow onions minced

2 cups worchestershire sauce

1/2 cup lemon juice

2 tablespoons dry mustard

2 cups vinegar

Directions

1. Clean ribs and set aside. Make marinade with garlic, molasses, apple cider vinegar and vegetable oil. Pour on ribs and marinate all night.
2. Discard marinade and season ribs with rub.
3. Prepare grill. In the meantime, add all barbeque sauce ingredients together. Cook on grill.
4. Mop ribs with barbeque sauce every 5 minutes.
5. Serve as sandwiches.

Sliced Pork Butt

(Number of servings 50; size of servings 1/2 pound)

Ingredients

4—5 pound pork butts

Rub

1/2 cup seasoning salt

2 pounds brown sugar

2 cups Kosher salt

1 cup cayenne pepper

2 gallons commercial barbeque sauce

Directions

1. Clean pork butts. Wash and pat dry. Set aside. In a large bowl, combine spices and rub evenly over meat. Wrap and refrigerate for 8 hours.

2. Grill for 5 hours and mop with barbeque sauce.
3. Slice and serve on buns.

Barbeque Wild Hog

(Number of serving-50; size of servings -1/4 pound)

Ingredients

1-15-20 pound wild hog

4 gallons apple cider vinegar

1 cup fresh rosemary, chopped

2 cups seasoning salt

1 gallon commercial barbeque sauce

Directions

1. Clean wild hog very well and add rosemary inside and soak in vinegar over night.
2. Discard vinegar and clean rosemary from cavity. Rub salt on outer portion.
3. Prepare smoker; Smoke pig for 24 hours or until desired doneness. Serve with commercial sauce.

Barbeque Pork Riblets

(Number of servings 50; size of servings — 1 sandwich)

Ingredients

25 pounds small tender spare ribs, cut into fours

1 cup each — seasoning salt, cumin, salt, black pepper, cayenne pepper and onion powder

2 gallons commercial barbeque sauce

10 loaves whole wheat bread

Directions

1. Clean and wash ribs. Set aside. In a large bowl combine together all seasonings.
2. Sprinkle over ribs. Prepare grill. Grill ribs until almost done on both sides.
3. Mop ribs with sauce and continue to cook.
4. Serve four ribs on each sandwich.

Shaved Smithfield Hams

(Number of servings 50; size of servings one sandwich)

Ingredients

2- 30 pounds Smithfield Hams

1 gallon honey

2 tablespoons mustard

10 cups pineapple juice

50 wheat buns

1 quart mustard

Directions

1. Trim ham. Grill for 8 hours.
2. Mix together honey, mustard and pineapple juice.
3. Pour over hams and bake for 2 additional hours. Remove hams from heat.
4. Cool. Shave hams into paper thin slices. Serve ham on wheat buns with mustard.

Boiled Chitterlings

50-1/2 cup Servings

Amount Ingredients

100 pounds Pork Chitterlings

10 (2 cups per pot) large onions, chopped

10 (2 cups per cup) celery, chopped

10 cloves(2 per pot) garlic, chopped

5 large (per pot) White potatoes

1 teaspoon per pot Thyme

1/2 teaspoon per pot Rosemary

1 cup per pot apple cider vinegar

10 tablespoons (2 Tablespoons per pot) red pepper flakes

10 Tablespoons (2 Tablespoons per pot) Salt

Directions

1. Clean chitterlings.
2. In five large pots, equally place chitterlings in each pot. Cover with water.
3. Add onions, celery, and red pepper flakes. Stir. Bring to a boil
4. Cook for 45 minutes and then add salt. Stir well.
5. Boil an additional 15 minutes.

Honey Baby Back Ribs

(Number of servings -50; Size of serving one sandwich)

Ingredients

15 pounds pork baby back ribs

Rub:

1 cup seasoning salt

1/2 gallon honey

1 quart apple cider vinegar

2 cups brown sugar

1 cup Worcestershire sauce

1/4 cup cayenne pepper

Directions

1. Parboil ribs until tender. Drain. Pat dry. Rub with salt.
2. In a large saucepan, combine remaining ingredients, Thinly mop ribs with sauce.
3. Grill until desired doneness. Continue to add sauce.
4. Serve on bread.

Memphis Barbeque Baby Back Ribs

Number of servings-50; size of servings 1/4 pound

Ingredients

40 pounds baby back ribs

Rub:

1 cup garlic powder

2 cups brown sugar

1/2 cup black pepper

1/4 cup salt

1 cup paprika

Directions for rub:

1. Pour all spices in a blender. Bled well for 10 minutes.
2. Rub on prepared meat.
3.

Direction for barbeque sauce

1 quart ketchup

1 quart tomato sauce

1 cup mustard

2 cups molasses

1 yellow onion, finely chopped

1 cup apple cider vinegar

3 garlic cloves

2 quarts water

Directions

1. In a large saucepot, combine all ingredients. Cover and cook slowly for one hour; stirring occasionally.
2. Cool and use to mop ribs.

Grilling meat:

1. Prepare meat and grill. Slowly grill until done.
2. Mop meat with barbeque sauce.
3. Grill until desired doneness.

Barbequed Pulled Pork

Number of servings -50; size of servings -one sandwich)

10—5 pound pork roasts

Rub:

2 tablespoons seasoning mix

1 tablespoon celery salt

1 tablespoon garlic salt

1 tablespoon onion powder

3 cups brown sugar

3 gallons commercial sweet barbeque sauce

10 loaves wheat bread

Directions

1. Clean and wash meat. Set aside. Combine the next five ingredients. Stir well.
2. Rub generously over meat. Place meat in aluminum pans.
3. Prepare smoker. Cook meat slowly until meat pulls away from roasts and the meat is Done.
4. Pull all meat from roasts and transfer to another pan. Pour barbeque sauce over meat And continue to cook to desired doneness.
   Serve on sandwiches

Crab Boil

(Number of servings; size of servings —1 sandwich)

Ingredients

3 package of Old Bay Seasonings

5 pounds red potatoes

3 pounds carrots cut into 1" lengths

5 pounds small onions

4 dozen eggs

3 stalks of celery, chopped

10 pounds small corn on the cob

1 cup seasoning salt

10 pounds shrimp

5 pounds beef sausages

10 pounds crabs

Directions

1. Using a large pot, fill with water and stir in Old Bay Seasoning. Boil for 30 minutes Potatoes, carrots, onions, eggs and celery. Stir well add more ingredients and stir in remaining Ingredients.
2. Cook for 25 minutes are until desired doneness. Serve.

Fried Catfish

(Number of Serving 50; Size of serving 2)

Ingredients

25 pounds whole catfish, cleaned and washed

5 pounds fish fry mix

2 cups seasoning salt

5 gallons peanut oil

Directions

1. Clean and wash catfish. Set aside.
2. Mix fish fry mix and seasoning salt together.
3. Coat each piece of fish well with mixture. Cover and refrigerate for 2 hours.
4. Heat oil and deep fry catfish until golden brown. Serve.

Fried Whiting

(Number of servings 50; size of serving 2 pieces)

Ingredients

25 pounds whiting fish

10 Pounds yellow corn meal

1 pound self-rising flour

3 cups salt

1 cup black pepper

1 cup garlic powder

5 gallons peanut oil

Directions

1. Clean and wash whiting. Set aside. In a large container, mix together Corn meal, flour, salt black pepper, and garlic powder.
2. Coat each piece of fish. Preheat oil to 350 degrees Fahrenheit.
3. Fry fish until golden brown.

Fried Tilapia

(Number of servings-50; size of servings 2 filets)

Ingredients

25 pounds Tilapia

5 pounds white cornmeal mix

1 cup seasoning salt

1 cup garlic salt

1 cup black pepper

1 cup dried parsley

1 cup onion powder

5 gallons peanut oil

Directions

1. Clean and wash tilapia. Separate into filets. Set aside.
2. In a large container, stir together corn meat mix, seasoning salt, Garlic salt, black pepper, dried parsley flakes, and onion powder.
3. Coat each filet with mixture. Preheat oil.
4. Deep fry fish in oil. Serve hot.

Fried Croaker

(Number of servings-50; size of serving is one piece of fish)

Ingredients

25 pounds whole croaker fish, cleaned and washed

2 cups salt

2 cups black pepper

2 cups seasoning salt

10 pounds yellow corn meal

5 gallons peanut oil

Directions

1. Clean and wash croaker fish. Season with salt, pepper and seasoning salt.
2. Coat with yellow meal. Preheat oil.
3. Fry in oil until golden brown. Serve.

Grilled Crab Cakes

10 pounds crab meat

10 eggs, beaten

3 tablespoons salt

2 tablespoons black pepper

2 cups onions, chopped finely

1 cup green peppers, chopped finely

10 cups cracker crumbs

2 cups worchestershire sauce

Directions

1. Mix together all ingredients. Make into 100 crab cakes.
2. Prepare grill. Grill until done. Serve

Dried Smoked Shrimp Kabobs

(Number of servings -50; size of servings —one kabob)

Ingredients

25 pounds Jumbo shrimp, cleaned and shucked

1 gallon soy sauce

50 wooden skewers

Directions

1. Clean and wash shrimp; leave tails on. Soak in soy sauce for 4 hours. Discard and wash Shrimp. Soak skewers in water. Thread shrimp on skewers. Prepare grill.
2. Grill shrimp until dried out. Serve.

Grilled Blackened Catfish

(Number of servings 50; size of servings — 1 filet)

Ingredients

12 pounds catfish

1 gallon Louisiana Blackened mix

Vegetable spray

Directions

1. Wash and pat catfish dry. Separate into 50 pieces.
2. Blacken fish until fully covered.
3. Prepare grill with vegetable spray and grill catfish until done

Low Country Boil

(Number of servings-50; size of servings -1 plate)

Ingredients

5 packages Old Bay Seasoning

5 pounds new potatoes

50 pieces corn cobbettes

15 pounds crab legs

10 pounds jumbo shrimp

10 pounds oysters

Directions

1. In a large pot, add water and stir in Old Bay Seasoning. Add potatoes and cook Until almost done. Add remaining ingredients and cook until desired doneness.
2. Serve in plate,

Salmon Patties

(Number of servings 50; size of serving —2 patties)

Ingredients

2(no.10) cans Salmon

10 eggs

5 pounds cracker crumbs

2 pounds onions, chopped

1 cup black pepper

1/2 cup salt

Directions

1. Open cans of salmon and drain. Flake salmon and remove black skin.
2. In large pan stir together all ingredients and make into 100 patties.
3. Refrigerate for 4 hours. Prepare grill. Grill on both sides.
4. Serve two patties per person.

Shrimp Po' Boys

(Number of servings -50; size of servings 1 sandwich)

Ingredients

12 pounds shrimp, picked and shelled and washed

5 pounds pancake mix

2quarts milk

1 tablespoon salt

2 quarts corn oil

50 hamburger buns

1 quart mayonnaise

3 heads iceberg lettuce, chopped

5 yellow onions, finely chopped

Directions

1. Prepare shrimp as directed. Set aside. Prepare pancake batter with milk.
2. Dip in batter. Preheat oil to 350 degrees. Fry shrimp for 8 to 10 minutes.
3. Drain. Toast buns on grill. Spread buns with mayonnaise add shrimp, lettuce and onions. Add shrimp. Serve

Smoked Salmon

(Number of servings -50; size of serving —one piece)

Ingredients

10 pounds salmon, cleaned and cut into fourths

5 gallons of brine

Directions

1. Soak salmon in brine over night
2. Discard brine and dry off salmon.
3. Prepare grill for smoking salmon. Spray grill with vegetable spray.
4. Grill until desired doneness. Serve.

Poultry

Barbequed Chicken Quarters

(Number of servings -50; size of servings; 1 leg quarter)

Ingredients

50 chicken leg quarters

Rub:

1 cup seasoning salt

1 cup black pepper

2 cups brown sugar

3 gallons commercial barbeque sauce

Directions

1. Wash chicken leg quarters and season meat.
2. Grill meat until done.
3. Brush with barbeque sauce.

Grilled Chicken Halves

(Number of servings -50; size of servings -1 half)

Ingredients

25-2 1/2 pound chickens - cut into halves

1 pound Mrs. Dash's seasonings

1 pound seasoning salt

Directions

1. Prepare chicken halves, wash and dry.
2. Season with seasonings and seasoning salt.
3. Cover and refrigerate for 4 hours.
4. Prepare grill and grill to desired doneness.

Deep-Fried Chicken

(Number of servings -50; size of servings —2 pieces)

Ingredients

25 pounds chicken pieces

10 pounds self-rising flour

1 cup black pepper

1 cup seasoning salt

10 gallons peanut oil

Directions
1. Clean and wash chicken. Set aside.
2. Mix together flour, black pepper and seasoning salt.
3. Coat chicken with flour.
4. Heat oil in deep fryer.
5. Fry chicken until golden brown.

ALABAMA A& M UNIVERSITY

Normal (near Huntsville), Alabama

MOTTO: "Service is Sovereignty."

HISTORY: Founded 1875 (Public University (Urban 880 acres) -Land Grant University)

ENROLLMENT: 6,000

DEGREES GRANTED: Bachelor's, Master's and Doctoral degrees

MASCOT: "Butch"

NICKNAME: Bulldogs/Lady Bulldogs

COLORS: Maroon and White

NAME OF STADIUM: Lewis Crews

NAME OF MARCHING BAND: The Marching Maroon and White Band _Show Band of the South

SPORTS: Basketball, Bowling, Cross-Country, Football, Golf,

Indoor Track, Outdoor Track, Softball, Tennis, Volleyball

CLASSIC BOWL GAMES: 1) MAGIC CITY CLASSIC —Alabama A & M University vs Alabama State University

2) CSRA CLASSIC —Savannah State University vs Alabama A&M University @ Augusta, GA

ALABAMA STATE UNIVERSITY

Montgomery, Alabama

Motto: "When we teach class, the world takes note."

HISTORY: Founded 1867 (Urban, Public, 172 acres)

ENROLLMENT: 5,600

DEGREES GRANTED: Bachelors and postgraduate degrees

MASCOT/NICKNAME: Hornets/ Lady Hornets

NAME OF MARCHING BAND: The Marching Hornets Band

SCHOOL COLORS: Old Gold and Black

SPORTS: Baseball, Basketball, Bowling, Cross-Country, Football, Golf, Indoor Track, Outdoor track, Soccer, Softball, Tennis, Volleyball

NANE OF STADIUM: Hornet Stadium

CLASSIC BOWL GAMES:

1) DETROIT CLASSIC — Florida A&M University vs Alabama State University @Detroit, MI

2) MAGIC CITY CLASSIC — Alabama A&M University vs Alabama State University @Legion Field Birmingham, AL

3) TURKEY DAY CLASSIC—Tuskegee University vs Alabama State University @Cramton Bowl Montgomery, AL

4) GOLF COAST CLASSIC-Alcorn State University vs. Alabama State University @ Mobile, Ala

ALCORN STATE UNIVERSITY

Lorman (Alcorn State), Mississippi

Motto: Service, Scholarship, Dignity

HISTORY: Founded 1871 (Public University-Land Grant University)

(established by Presbyterians Church, 1700 acres)

ENROLLMENT: 3,443

DEGREES GRANTED: Bachelors and Masters Degrees

SCHOOL COLORS: Purple and Gold

MASCOT/NICKNAME: Braves/Lady Braves

NAME OF MARCHING BAND: The Alcorn Sounds of Dynamite

NAME OF STADIUM: Jack Spinks Stadium

SPORTS: Baseball, Basketball, Cross-Country, Football, Golf,

Indoor Track, Outdoor Track, Soccer, Softball, Tennis, Volleyball

CLASSIC BOWL GAMES:

GULF COAST CLASSIC

Alcorn University vs. Alabama State University @Mobile, Ala

Capital City Classic —Alcorn State vs Jackson State University Jackson, Mississippi

ARKANSAS CLASSIC

University of Arkansas @Pine Bluff vs Alcorn State University

Golden Lion Stadium, Pine Bluff, Arkansas

GRAMBLING STATE UNIVERSITY

GRAM BLING, LOU ISANA

MOTTO: "Where Everybody is Somebody."

HISTORY: Founded 1901 (Rural/Public)

ENROLLMENT: 4,988

DEGREES GRANTED: Bachelors and Postgraduate degrees

SCHOOL COLORS: Black and Gold

MASCOT/NICKNAME: Tigers

NAME OF MARCHING BAND: Grambling State University Tiger Band

NAME OF STADIUM: Robinson Stadium

SPORTS: Baseball, Basketball, Cross-Country, Football, Golf, outdoor track, soccer, softball, tennis, volleyball

CLASSSIC BOWL GAMES: 1) RED RIVER CLASSIC—Grambling University vs University Arkansas At Pine Bluff @ Shreveport, Louisiana

2) STATE FAIR CLASSIC —Prairie View A&M vs Grambling @ Cotton Bowl

Dallas, Texas

3) BAYOU CLASSIC — Southern, Baton Rouge vs Grambling sponsored by

State Farm Insurance Company @New Orleans, La.

JACKSON STATE UNIVERSITY

1400 Lynch Street

Jackson, Mississippi 39217

Motto: "Challenging Minds. Changing Lives."

HISTORY: Founded 1877 (Public University)

ENROLLMENT: 8,351

DEGREES GRANTED: Bachelor's, master's, and doctoral degrees

SCHOOL COLORS: Royal Blue and White

Mascot/Nickname: Tigers/Lady Tigers

NAME OF BAND: The Sonic Boom of the South

NAME OF STADIUM: Mississippi Veterans Memorial Stadium

SPORTS: Baseball, Basketball, Cross-Country, Football, Golf, Outdoor track, Softball, Volleyball.

CLASSIC BOWL GAMES: 1) Southern Heritage Classic-Tennessee State University vs

Jackson State University @Memphis, Tenn.

2) CAPITAL CITY CLASSIC — Alcorn State University vs Jackson State University @ Jackson, Ms.

3) CIRCLE CITY CLASSIC- Florida A&M vs Jackson State Univ @ Indianapolis, IN.

4) MEAC/SWAC CHALLENGE KICK-OFF ESPN2 — Hampton University vs Jackson State University —Florida Citrus Bowl

MISSISSIPPI VALLEY STATE UNIVERSITY

14000 Highway 82 West

ITTA BENA, MISSISSIPPI 38942

HISTORY: Founded 1950 (Type Public University-Campus rural)

ENROLLMENT: 2,500 students

DEGREES GRANTED: Bachelor degrees

COLORS: Forest Green and White

MASCOT/NICKNAME: Delta Devils/Devilettes

STADIUM: Rice - Totten Stadium

SPORTS: FOOTBALL, BASKETBALL, cross-country, golf, tennis, track, soccer, volleyball, softball, bowling

CLASSIC BOWL GAMES:

PRAIRIE VIEW A & M UNIVERSITY

Prairie View, Texas

MOTTO: Prairie View Producers of Productive People."

HISTORY: Founded 1876 (Rural Univeristy-1449 acres —Land Grant University, Public)

ENROLLMENT: 8,608

DEGREES GRANTED: Bachelors and Masters Degrees

SCHOOL COLORS: PURPLE AND GOLD

MASCOT/NICKNAME: Panthers/Lady Panthers

NAME OF MARCHING BAND: The Prairie View A&M University Marching Storm NAME OF STADIUM: Blackshear Field

SPORTS: Baseball, Basketball, Bowling, Golf, Football, Tennis, Softball, Soccer, Volleyball, Tennis,

CLASSIC BOWL GAMES: 1) STATE FAIR CLASSIC — Prairie View A & M vs. Grambling University @Cotton Bowl at Dallas, Texas

SOUTHERN UNIVERSITY

Baton Rouge, Louisiana

MOTTO: "A people's institution serving the state, the nation and the world."

HISTORY: Founded 1879 (1880) (Public University-Land-Grant Institution)

ENROLLMENT: 8,900 students

DEGREES GRANTED: Bachelors and postgraduate degrees

SCHOOL COLORS: Columbia Blue and Gold

MASCOT/NICKNAME: Jaguars and Lady Jaguars

NAME OF STADIUM: A.W. MUNFORD STADIUM

NAME OF MARCHING BAND: The Human Jukebox

SPORTS: Baseball, Basketball, Cross [Country Football, Indoor-Track, Soccer, Tennis

CLASSIC BOWL GAMES: 1) LAS VEGAS CLASSIC _ Southern University vs North Carolina A&T Univ.@Sam Boyd Stadium Las Vegas, NV

2) BAYOU CLASSIC - Southern University vs Grambling University Sponsored by State Farm Insurance @New Orleans

TEXAS SOUTHERN UNIVERSITY

Houston, Texas

HISTORY: Founded 1947 (Public, Urban University)

ENROLLMENT: 9,500 students

DEGREES GRANTED: Bachelors and postgraduate degrees

SCHOOL COLORS: Maroon and Gray

MASCOT/NICKNAME: Tigers

NAME OF MARCHING BAND: Ocean of Soul

NAME OF STADIUM: Alexander Durley Complex (Primary), Reliant Stadium (Secondary)

SPORTS: baseball, basketball, cross country, football, golf, indoor track, outdoor tract & field and tennis, soccer, softball, volleyball.

CLASSIC BOWL GAMES: 1) LABOR DAY CLASSIC —Prairie View A&M University vs Texas Southern University @ Reliant Stadium, Houston, Texas

2) ROSE CITY CLASSIC —Texas College vs. Texas Southern College @ Tyler, Texas

3) CAPITAL CITY CLASSIC — Texas Southern University vs Shaw University @ Sacramento, California

♦ ♦ ♦

UNIVERSITY OF ARKANSAS AT PINE BLUFF

Pine Bluff, Arkansas

HISTORY: Founded 1873 (Type Public, Urban University; Land-Grant University)

ENROLLMENT: 3,323 students

DEGREES GRANTED: Bachelors and postgraduate degrees

MASCOT/NICKNAME: Golden Lions/Lionettes

COLORS: Black and Gold

NAME OF MARCHING BAND: The Musical Machine of the Mid South

NAME OF STADIUM: Golden Lion Stadium

SPORTS: Baseball, Basketball, Bowling, Cross —Country, Indoor Track, Outdoor Track, Football, Golf, Softball, Track, Tennis

CLASSIC BOWL GAMES: 1) RED RIVER CLASSIC —Grambling University vs University of Arkansas At Pine Bluff @ Shreveport, Louisiana

DESSERTS/MEAC

MEAC CONFERENCE

CONFERENCE MEMBERS:

BETHUNE – COOKMAN –Daytona, Florida-Wilcats

DELAWARE STATE-Dover, Delaware-Hornets

FLORIDA A&M-Tallahassee, Florida, Rattlers

HAMPTON UNIVERSITY-Hampton, Virginia-Pirates

HOWARD UNIVERSITY –WASHINGTON,DC –Bisons

MORGAN STATE- Baltimore, Maryland -Bears

NORFOLK STATE- Norfolk, Virginia - Spartans

NORTH CAROLINA A&T- Greensboro, North Carolina -Aggies

SAVANNAH STATE UNIVERSITY -, Savannah, Georgia -TIGERS

SOUTH CAROLINA STATE UNIVERSITY- Orangeburg, South Carolina, Bulldogs

SUGGESTED TAILGATING DESSERT RECIPES

Apple Cobbler

Number of servings -50; Size of servings =1/2 cup

Ingredients

3-9 inch pie crusts, rolled into strips

2-(number 10) apple pie filling

1 cup sugar

1 cup brown sugar

1 tablespoon cinnamon

2 cups butter, melted

11/2 teaspoons salt

Directions

1. Line on the bottom of two-large aluminum pans with half of pie crust strips. Set aside. In a large sauce pan, combine together apple pie filling, sugars, cinnamon, butter and salt.
2. Evenly distribute the filling into pans. Cover with the remaining pie crust strips.
3. Bake in oven at 350 degrees until browned. Remove from oven. Cover with foil.
4. Keep hot on grill until serving at tailgating event.

Bread Pudding

Number of servings 50; Size of servings 1/2 cup

Ingredients

3 loaves white bread, cubed

2 quarts homogenized milk

2 (303 cans) evaporated milk

6 eggs, whipped

2 tablespoons vanilla flavoring

2 teaspoons cinnamon

3 cups sugar

1 cup brown sugar

4 cups raisins

Directions

1. In a large 2 gallon mixing bowl, soak bread cubes into homogenized and evaporated milk until disintegrated. Stir in remaining ingredients.
2. Cook in 4- 13inch X 9 inch pans at 350 degrees F until golden brown.
3. Cool. Cut into squares. Serve on small 6 inch plates.

Buttermilk Chess Pie

Number of servings- 50; Size of servings - 1 tart

Ingredients

2 dozen large eggs

10 cups sugar

2 1/2 cups butter, melted

1 cup white cornmeal

1 quart buttermilk

1 1/2 tablespoons vanilla extract cup vinegar

50 miniature pie tart shells

Directions

1. In a large bowl, whisk together the eggs, sugar, melted butter, cornmeal, butter milk, salt, vanilla and vinegar. Blend well.
2. Pour into individual tarts. Place on baking sheets. Do not crowd.
3. Bake about ten at a time. Bake at 350 for 30 minutes or until done.

Cherry Cobbler

Number of servings SO; Size of servings 1/2 cup

Ingredients

2— (Number 10 cans) cherry pie filling

2 1/2 cups sugar

1 tablespoon vanilla

2 cups water

1 teaspoon almond flavor

Topping:

5 cups flour, self-rising

2 cups sugar

1 cup brown sugar

2 teaspoons cinnamon

4 eggs, beaten

2 cups milk

2 cups butter, melted

Directions

1. Preheat oven to 375 degrees. In a large bowl, mix together cherry pie filling, sugar, vanilla and water. Pour into a large aluminum pan. Set aside.
2. In a large bowl, combine flour, sugar, baking powder, cinnamon, eggs, milk and butter. Beat well. Spread topping over cherry filling.
3. Cook in oven until browned. Cover with aluminum foil. Keep hot on grill until ready to serve.

Chocolate Krispies

Number of serving 50 Size of serving -1 square

Ingredients

1 large box graham crackers cereal

1 large bag miniature marshmallows

2 cups pecan, chopped

1 large bag semi —sweet chocolate

Directions

1. In a large pan, mix together cereal, marshmallows and pecans. Set aside.
2. Melt chocolate chips on grill in a large pan stirring constantly until well melted.
3. Mix well with cereal mixture. Smooth into aluminum foil and cut into 50 small squares. Serve in small

bags.

Coconut Patties

(Number of servings 50; size of serving 1 patty)

10 cups sugar

11 1/4 cups sweetened condensed milk

1 quart water

10 cups coconut

2 tablespoons vanilla

5 cups nuts, chopped

2 cups butter

Directions

1. Add together sugar, condensed milk and water. Stir together. Boil to a temperature 234- 238 degrees). Cool to room temperature.
2. Add coconut and nuts. Add butter and vanilla. Drop on wax paper in small pats.

Individual Coconut Pecan Pies

(Number of servings 50; size of servings 1 tart)

Ingredients

50 individual tart shells, plain

12 cups dark molasses

8 cups sugar

2 cups butter

3 tablespoons vanilla

4 10 cups pecans, chopped

5 8 cups, flaked coconuts

Directions

Directions

1. Preheat oven to 350 degrees. Separate tart shells into baking sheets.
2. Set aside. In a large container, pour molasses and sugar.
3. Cook over low heat until sugar dissolves.
4. Remove from heat and cool down.
5. Beat eggs for 5 minutes. Gradually add syrup to eggs and beat well after each addition.
6. Be careful; eggs will curdle. Beat in butter and vanilla.
7. Add nuts and coconut. Pour into tart shells. Bake for 45 minutes at 350 degrees. Careful Do not let tarts burn.

Oatmeal Cookies

(Number of servings -50; size of servings 2 cookies)

Ingredients

6 cups flour, self rising

3 cups light brown sugar

2 cups butter, softened

4 eggs

2 tablespoons vanilla

2 pounds pecans, chopped

3 cups molasses

10 cups old-fashioned rolled oats

Directions

1. In a large bowl, add flour, sugar, butter and eggs. Stir well. Gradually add in vanilla, nuts and molasses. Stir in oats, small amount at a time. Roll into 1" balls. Flatten with fork. Place foil on the grill and grill until done or bake at 350 degrees for 8 to 10 minutes until done.

Lemon Tarts

(Number of servings 50; size of servings; 1 tart)

Ingredients

50 Individual tart shells

10 cups lemon pudding mix

Directions

1. Separate tart shells. Brown shells in a preheated 400 degrees oven. Do not burn. Set aside
2. Prepare lemon pudding mix as indicated on box.
3. Pour into shells. Let set. Refrigerate until time to serve.

Peach Cobbler

50 Servings — 1/2 Cup Servings

Amount   Ingredients

10 Pounds Peaches, Peeled And Sliced

6 Cups Sugar

3 Cups Butter

2 Tablespoons Cinnamon

2 Tablespoons Vanilla Extract

1 Teaspoon Salt

1 Tablespoon Cornstarch

2 Rolls -4 Flats Each Pastry Dough

Directions

1. Peel and slice peaches and place in a big saucepan add 1 gallon of water. Stir. Bring to a boil. Stir in sugar. Add sugar and cook until tender about 5 more minutes.
2. And the remaining ingredients and cook for 5 minutes.
3. Line 4 large aluminum pans (13 X 9 X 2) with one layer of crust per pan. Prick the crust.
4. Evenly distribute the peach pie filling per pan. Place top on each pie filling.
5. Prick the top and cook 40 minutes or until desired doneness. Cool. Cover
6. For tailgating: Keep warm on grill for serving hot; for cold keep in cooler then serve.

Pound Cake

Amount For 50 Servings -4 Pound Cakes

Amount   Ingredients

6 Pounds Butter

18 Cups Sugar

24 Eggs

6 Cups Whole Milk

15 Cups Flour Sifted

3 Teaspoons Salt

15 Teaspoons Baking Powder

5 Teaspoons Vanilla Flavoring

2 Teaspoons Lemon Flavoing

2 Teaspoons Almond Flavoring

Directions

1. In a large mixer, cream together butter and sugar; gradually add in eggs one At a time. Beat well after each addition. Set aside.
2. Sift together flour, salt and baking powder.
3. Add alternately flour and milk to the egg mixture.
4. Beat batter well.
5. Gradually add in flavorings. Stir well.
6. Grease 4 tube cake pans. Pour cake batter in cake pans and bake in a 300 oven until Cake is done. It will probably take about 35-40 minutes,

Virginia Peach Bread Amount 4 loaves

Amount   Ingredients

2 Pounds Butter

1 Cup Sugar

5 Eggs

10 Cups Flour, Self Rising

3 Cups Milk

2 Cups Nuts, Chopped

1 (No. 2 1/2 Can) Peach Slices, Diced

Directions

1. Cream together butter and sugar.

2. Gradually add in eggs, one at a time.
3. Stir in flour and milk alternately.
4. Stir in nuts and diced peaches.
5. Grease 4 aluminum loaf pans. Pour batter equally in pans.
6. Bake each loaf for an hour.

Pecan Brownies

50- 2 servings each

Amount   Ingredients

10 cups flour

2 cups cocoa

3 tablespoons baking powder

1 tablespoon salt

3 cups butter, softened

5 eggs

4 cups sugar

3 cups milk

2 tablespoons   vanilla extract

4 cups nuts, chopped

Directions

1. SIFT TOGETHER FLOUR, COCOA, BAKING POWDER AND SALT. SET ASIDE.
2. CREAM TOGETHER BUTTER, EGGS and sugar. Add eggs one at a time.
3. GRADUALLY ADD MILK AND FLOUR TO CREAMED BUTTER AND SUGAR MIXTURE,

4. ADD IN NUTS AND VANILLA.
5. Grease 2- large pans -11x 15 pans. Equally pour batter in pans,
6. Bake at 350 degrees F for 40 minutes or until done. Cool.
7. Cut into 2 inch squares. Wrap in clear wrap. Serve.

Strawberry Tarts

Size of Serving; 1 per person

50 graham cracker tarts

6 pounds strawberries sliced

2 pounds sugar

1 1/2 cup Cornstarch

1 1/2 tablespoons vanilla

Directions

1. Stem and wash strawberries. Cut in half.
2. Place strawberries in a large pot add 2 quarts of water to pot.
3. Bring to a boil. Stir well. Gradually add in sugar.
4. Cook until all sugar is dissolved. Stir Until mixture thickens. Add vanilla extract And red food color. Stir and Cook for 5 additional minutes.

Grilled Peach Halves

50-1/2 peach

Amounts   Ingredients

25 large peaches, cut—into halves

2 cups butter, melted

4 cups dark brown sugar

5 cups nuts, finely chopped

Directions

1. Wash and cut peaches into halves. Remove seeds. Discard seeds. Wipe peaches dry. Peaches maybe peeled or skin left on.
1. Brush each peach half with butter. Sprinkle heavily With brown sugar and add nuts.
2. Grill until sugar melts. Cool and Serve.

Walnut Tarts

Size of serving — 1 pie tart

Amount   Ingredients

50 plain crust pie tarts

4 cups dark karo syrup

4 cups butter

4 cups dark brown sugar

10 eggs, large

2 tablespoons vanilla extract

5 pounds english walnuts, chopped

Directions

1. Separate all tarts and place on flat pans. Set aside,
2. In a large mixer, mix together syrup, butter, sugar and eggs. Stir well.
3. Add vanilla and walnuts. Stir well.
4. Pour into individual pie tarts and bake at 375 until done.
5. Cool and serve.

Goat Milk Ice Cream (Optional Peach Ice Cream)

Size of servings — 50-1/2 cup

amount ingredients

8 1/2 quarts goat milk, pasturized

7 eggs, large

4 cups sugar

2 tablespoons vanilla

1 quart Regular milk

Directions

1. In a large stockpot, place together all ingredients. Stir well.
2. Cook stirring well for about 15 minutes.
3. Cool. Freeze using ice cream freezer.
4. To make peach ice cream, stir in 2 quarts of diced peaches to mixture before freezing.

Sweet Potato Pie Tarts

50-1 tart per person

Amount   Ingredients

10 pounds Sweet potatoes, cooked and mashed

5 cups evaporated milk

6 cups sugar

2 cups   dark brown sugar

5 eggs, slightly beaten

2 tablespoons   cinnamon

1/2 cup vanilla extract

50 tarts plain pie crust

Directions

1. Wash and peel potatoes. Cover with water and cook until done. Drain and mash. Cool.
2. Add to mashed sweet potatoes the remaining ingredients. Stir well. Fill each tart with the sweet potato mixture.
3. Place tarts on cookie sheets and bake in oven for 30 minutes or until done.
4. Serve hot or cold.

Carmel Apples

50 Servings -1 Carmel Apple Per Person

Amount   Ingredients

52 delcious apples

50 cups caramel candies

1 pint   homogenized milk

50 ice cream —skewers

2 boxes wax paper

Directions

1. Wash apples and remove all stems. Dry and place skewers in top of apples and push each skewer from the top to almost one inch from the bottom of each apple. Set aside.
2. In a large saucepot, melt caramels over low heat. Stir in milk. Stir until The mixture reaches a medium thick consistency. Coat each apple with mixture.
3. Place apples about four inches apart. Cool before serving.

BETHUNE COOKMAN

640 Dr. Mary McLeod Bethune Blvd

Daytona Beach, FL

HISTORY: Founded 1904

ENROLLMENT-4,000

DEGREES GRANTED: bachelor and master degrees

SCHOOL COLORS: Maroon and Gold

Nickname: Wildcats

Mascot: Wil D Cat

NAME OF BAND: THE MARCHING WILDCATS OF BETHUNE-COOKMAN

NAME OF STADIUM: Municipal Stadium

Sports: Baseball, Basketball, Cross-Country, Softball, Tennis, golf

CLASSIC BOWL GAMES: 50th Gateway Classic

Bethune Cookman vs. Savannah State

GULF COAST CLASSIC

2) Bethune-Cookman vs Alabama State

3) Florida Classic –Bethune Cookman vs Florida A&M

At Municipal Stadium, Orlando Fl

DELAWARE STATE UNIVERSITY

DOVER, DELWARE

MOTTO: "Making our mark on the world"

HISTORY: 1891(land-grant institution)

ENROLLMENT: 3,700

DEGREES GRANTED: bachelor's degrees and master degrees

SCHOOL COLORS: Columbia Red and Blue

Nickname: Hornets

NAME OF BAND: The Approaching Storm

Name of Stadium: Alumni Stadium

SPORTS: Baseball, Basketball, cross-country, football, Track, Soccer, Softball, Tennis, volleyball, wrestling.

FLORIDA A & M UNIVERSITY (FAMU)

Tallahassee, Florida

MOTTO: Excellence With Caring

HISTORY: Founded 1887 (Land-Grant Institution)

ENROLLMENT: 13,089

DEGREES GRANTED: 62 bachelor's degrees in 103 majors, 36 master's degrees, two professional degrees and eleven doctoral degrees

SCHOOL COLORS: Orange and Green

NICKNAME/MASCOT: Rattlers/Lady Rattlers

NAME OF THE MARCHING BAND: The Marching 100

NAME OF STADIUM: Fort Bragg Memorial Stadium

SPORTS: Baseball, Basketball, Cross-country, Football, Golf, Outdoor track, Softball, Tennis, Volleyball, Track and Field, Aquatics

CLASSIC BOWL GAMES: 1) ORANGE BLOSSUM CLASSIC-Florida A&M University vs South Carolina University @Fort Bragg Stadium, Tallahassee, FL

2) ATLANTA FOOTBALL CLASSIC-Tennessee State University vs Florida A & M University @ Atlanta, Ga

3) FLORIDA CLASSIC –Florida A&M University vs Bethune-Cookman University @Orlando, Fl.

4) FLORIDA CLASSIC – Florida A&M University vs Alabama State University @ Detroit, Michigan

5) CIRCLE CITY CLASSIC – Florida A& M University vs Jackson State University @ Indianapolis, IN sponsored by Coca-Cola

HAMPTON UNIVERSITY

Hampton, VA

MOTTO: The Standards of Excellence; An education for Life.

HISTORY: Founded 1868 (Normal Hampton Institute in 1924 and Hampton University in 1984

First building established in 1870.)

(Emancipation Proclamation was read under a tree known as Emancipation Oak)

ENROLLMENT: Undergraduates 4500.

NAME OF STADIUM: Armstrong Stadium

NICKNAME/MASCOT: Pirates

SCHOOL COLORS: Royal Blue and white

SPORTS: Baseball, Basketball, Football, Tennis, Track Indoor and Outdoor, Volleyball, Bowling, Golf, Sailing, Softball

CLASSIC BOWL GAMES: 1) NEW YORK URBAN LEAGUE CLASSIC-Morgan State and Hampton University @New Jersey Meadlowlands Stadium

2) BATTLE OF THE BAY CLASSIC –Hampton University vs Norfolk State University @Norfolk, Virginia 3) RIVERFRONT CLASSIC –Hampton University vs Tuskegee University @Cleveland Brown Stadium Cleveland, Ohio

3)MEAC/SWAC CHALLENGE KICK-OFF ESPN2 –Hampton University vs Jackson State University Florida Citrus Bowl

HOWARD UNIVERSITY

WASHINGTON, D.C.

MOTTO: Veritas et Utilitas (Truth and Service)

HISTORY: Founded 1867 (Private-Urban-258 acres)

ENROLLMENT: 11,850

DEGREES GRANTED: Bachelors, masters. Doctoral degrees and professional degrees in

Pharmacy, law, medicine, dentistry and divinity.

SCHOOL COLORS: Red, White and White

NICKNAME/MASCOT: Bison

NAME OF BAND: Howard University 'Showtime' Marching Band

NAME OF STADIUM: William H. Greene

SPORTS: Basketball, swimming, volleyball, tennis, soccer, football

CLASSIC BOWL GAMES:

MORGAN STATE UNIVERSITY

1700 EAST Cold Spring Lane

BALTIMORE, MARYLAND

MOTTO: "Gateway to Excellence"

HISTORY: Founded in 1867 (Trained men for the ministry)

ENROLLMENT: 7,500

Bachelor of Arts and Bachelor of Science degrees: Business, Engineering, Education, Architecture, Social Work, Hospitality Management and Arts and Sciences.

NAME OF STADIUM: Hughes Stadium

Sports: Basketball, Bowling, Cross Country, Football, Track and Field, Softball, Tennis, Volleyball

SCHOOL COLORS: Blue and Orange

NICKNAME/MASCOT: Bears

MARCHING BAND: Magnificent Marching Machine

CLASSIC BOWL GAMES: Whitney Young/Urban League Classic Morgan State University vs Hampton (New Jersey Mead Stadium)

2) NEW YORK URBAN LEAGUE CLASSIC Hampton vs Morgan State University

NORFOLK STATE UNIVERSITY

NORFOLK, VIRGINIA

MOTTO: "Achieving with Excellence"

FOUNDED: 1935 (Public, URBAN CAMPUS-134 ACRES)

ENROLLMENT: 6,200

DEGREES GRANTED; two associates, two doctoral degrees, 33 baccalaureate degrees, 16 master's degrees: Business, Education, Liberal Arts, Sciences and Technology, Social Work, Graduate Studies.

NICKNAME/MASCOT: Spartans

SCHOOL COLORS: Green and Gold

NAME OF STADIUM: William "Dick Price" Stadium

NAME OF MARCHING BAND: Spartan Legion

Sports: Baseball, Basketball, Bowling, Cross-Country, football, Track & Field, Softball, Tennis, Volleyball.

CLASSIC BOWL GAMES: 1) BATTLE OF THE BAY CLASSIC - Hampton University vs Norfolk State University @ Norfolk State 2) VIRGINIA LOTTERY LABOR DAY CLASSIC –Norfolk State University

Vs Virginia State University @ Norfolk State University 3) JOE TURNER CLASSIC- Savannah State University vs Norfolk State University @ Savannah, GA

4) FISH BOWL CLASSIC - Norfolk State University v s North Carolina A@T University @ Norfolk State University 5) BATTLE OF THE BAY CLASSIC- Hampton University vs Norfolk State University

NORTH CAROLINA AGRICULTURAL AND TECHNICAL STATE UNIVERSITY

GREENSBORO, NORTH CAROLINA

MOTTO: Mens et Manus (Mind and Hand)

HISTORY: Founded 1891 (Land-grant institution 692 acres main and agricultural campuses)

ENROLLMENT: 11,348

DEGREES GRANTED: Baccalaureate, master's, doctoral levels from two programs and six schools: Arts and Sciences, Engineering, Agriculture, Business and Economics, Education, Nursing, Technology and Graduate Studies.

NICKNAME: Aggies

MASCOT: bULLDOG

SCHOOL COLORS: Aggies Blue and Gold

NAME OF THE MARCHING BAND: The Marching Blue and Gold Machine Band

NAME OF STADIUM: Aggie Stadium or Sam Boyd

SPORTS: Baseball, Basketball, bowling, Cross Country, Football, Track & Field, Softball, Swimming, Tennis.

CLASSIC BOWL GAMES: 1) AGGIE-EAGLES CLASSIC – North Carolina Central University vs. North Carolina A&T University

2)LAS VEGAS CLASSIC – North Carolina A&T vs. Southern University 3) FISH BOWL CLASSIC- North Carolina A & T University vs. Norfolk State University

NORTH CAROLINA CENTRAL UNIVERSITY

Durham, North Carolina

MOTTO: Truth and Service

History: Founded in 1910 (Public, Urban,)

ENROLLMENT: 8,500 STUDENTS

Degrees Granted: baccalaureate, master's professional and doctoral degrees.

SCHOOL COLORS: Maroon and gray

Nickname/Mascot: Eagles

STADIUM: O'Kelley –Riddick Stadium

SPORTS: Baseball, Basketball, Cross-Country, Football, Softball, Tennis, Track and Field, Volleyball

CLASSIC BOWL GAMES: 1) AGGIES –EAGLES CLASSIC –North Carolina A & T vs North Carolina Central

SAVANNAH STATE UNIVERSITY

Savannah, Georgia

MOTTO: Lux Et. Veritas (Light and Truth)

History: Founded 1890 (Oldest public HBCU in Georgia_

Enrollment: 3, 820

Degrees Granted: bachelor's and Master's degrees

School Colors: Brunt Orange and Reflex Blue

Nickname/Mascot: Tigers

Name of Marching Band: Tigers Band

Name of Stadium: Ted Wright Stadium

Sports: Baseball, Basketball, football, indoor track, outdoor tract, track and field, softball, volleyball, golf

CLASSIC BOWL GAMES:

GATEWAY CLASSIC – Savannah State vs Bethune Cookman Alltel Stadium Jacksonville, Florida

Joe Turner Classic Savannah State University vs Norfolk State University Savannah, Georgia

MUSIC CITY CLASSIC Savannah State University vs Albany State University-Macon, GA

CSRA CLASSIC – Savannah State University vs Alabama A&M Univ Augusta, GA.

SOUTH CAROLINA STATE UNIVERSITY

ORANGEBURG, SOUTH CAROLINA

HISTORY: Founded 1896 (169 acre campus)

ENROLLMENT: 4,700 Students

MASCOT: Bulldog

DEGREES GRANTED: Sixty baccalaureate programs in Applied Professional Sciences, Biology, Education, Business, Engineering and Technology, Arts and Humanities.

NAME OF MARCHING BAND: MARCHING 101 BAND

SPORTS: Basketball, Bowling, Cross Country, Football, Golf, Track and Field, Soccer, Softball, Tennis, Volleyball.

CLASSIC BOWL GAMES: 1) –Tennessee State University vs. South Carolina State University @ Nashville, TN

2) SOUTHERN HERTIAGE CLASSIC –Tennessee State University v s Jackson State University @ Memphis, Tenn 3) CAPITAL CITY PALMETTO CLASSIC South Carolina State University Vs. Benedict College @ Columbia, SC 4) ORANGE BLOSSUM CLASSIC –Florida A&M University Vs South Carolina State University Fort Bragg Stadium , Tallahassee, Florida

INDEPENDENT COLLEGES
AND UNIVERSITIES

CENTRAL STATE UNIVERSITY WILBERFORCE, OHIO
CHEYNEY UNIVERSITY -CHEYNEY, PENN-WOLVES
LINCOLN UNIVERSITY -LINCOLN, MISSOURI, LIONS
LANGSTON UNIVERSITY, Langston, Oklahoma, Lions
TENNESSEE STATE UNIVERSITY
NASHVILLE, TENNESSEE -Tigers
TEXAS COLLEGE, TYLER, TEXAS STEERS
WEST VIRGINIA STATE UNIVERSITY INSTITUTE,
WEST VIRGINIA, YELLOW JACKETS
EDWARD WATERS COLLEGE -JACKSONVILLE,
FLORIDA, TIGERS/LADY TIGERS

HOMECOMING SPIRITS/
INDEPENDENTS

Suggested Recipes for Homecoming Spirits

Apple Wine Recipe

Ingredients

5 lbs. of Rome Beauty Apples

2 qts. Water

2 lbs. Sugar

1 pkg. Yeast Nutrient

1 pkg. Wine Yeast

Directions

1. Prepare fruit by peeling, removing cores and wasb fruit, chop into small pieces.
2. Boil water and cool, add sugar, stir until sugar is dissolved.
3. Add sugar water and fruit to five gallon crock. Cover for 24 hours.
4. Add yeast nutrient, wine yeast to the mixture stir with a wooden spoon. Cover and keep in a 70 degree place for three days.
5. Strain off the liquid with a cheese cloth into a gallon jug. Put an air lock on the end of the jug.
6. Place in a dry cool place 65 degrees F. for three weeks.
7. Siphon the wine off the sedimentation. Do not mix.
8. Place in clean jug and continue the process until fermentation ceases.
9. The fermentation has ceased when wine is clear.
10. Siphon off wine and place into wine bottles.

11. Place in wine bottles and cork; leave upright for three days and store on sides in racks for six months.

Apple/Cherry Wine Recipe

Ingredients

1 gallon granny smith apples

3 qts. Cherries

2 lbs. Granulated sugar

1 gal. Water

1 pkg. Wine Yeast

1 pkg. Yeast Nutrient

Directions

1. Prepare fruit by peeling, removing cores and wash fruit, chop into small pieces.
2. Boil water and cool, add sugar, stir until sugar is dissolved.
3. Add sugar water and fruit to five gallon crock. Cover for 24 hours.
4. Add yeast nutrient, wine yeast to the mixture stir with a wooden spoon. Cover and keep in a 70 degree place for three days.
5. Strain off the liquid with a cheese cloth into a gallon jug. Put an air lock on the end of the jug.
6. Place in a dry cool place 65 degrees F. for three weeks.
7. Siphon the wine off the sedimentation. Do not mix.
8. Place in clean jug and continue the process until fermentation ceases.
9. The fermentation has ceased when wine is clear.
10. Siphon off wine and place into wine bottles.

11. Place in wine bottles and cork; leave upright for three days and store on sides in racks for six months.

Apple/Pear Wine Recipe

Ingredients

1 gal. Rome beady apples, cored and diced

1 gal. Yellow pears, cored and diced

1 gal. Water

2 lbs. Granulated sugar

1 pkg. yeast nutrient

1 pkg. wine yeast

Directions

1. Prepare fruit by peeling, removing cores and wash fruit, chop into small pieces.
2. Boil water and cool, add sugar, stir until sugar is dissolved.
3. Add sugar water and fruit to five gallon crock. Cover for 24 hours.
4. Add yeast nutrient, wine yeast to the mixture stir with a wooden spoon. Cover and keep in a 70 degree place for three days.
5. Strain off the liquid with a cheese cloth into a gallon jug. Put an air lock on the end of the jug.
6. Place in a dry cool place 65 degrees F. for three weeks.
7. Siphon the wine off the sedimentation. Do not mix.
8. Place in clean jug and continue the process until fermentation ceases.
9. The fermentation has ceased when wine is clear.
10. Siphon off wine and place into wine bottles.

11. Place in wine bottles and cork; leave upright for three days and store on sides in racks for six months.

Apples/Blackberry and Elderberries Wine Recipe

Ingredients

2 lbs. Apples

2 lbs. Blackberries

1 lb. Elderberries

1 gal. Water

1 pkg. Yeast Nutrient

1 pkg. Wine Yeast

Directions

1. Prepare fruit by peeling, removing cores and wash fruit, chop into small pieces.
2. Boil water and cool, add sugar, stir until sugar is dissolved.
3. Add sugar water and fruit to five gallon crock. Cover for 24 hours.
4. Add yeast nutrient, wine yeast to the mixture stir with a wooden spoon. Cover and keep in a 70 degree place for three days.
5. Strain off the liquid with a cheese cloth into a gallon jug. Put an air lock on the end of the jug.
6. Place in a dry cool place 65 degrees F. for three weeks.
7. Siphon the wine off the sedimentation. Do not mix.
8. Place in clean jug and continue the process until fermentation ceases.
9. The fermentation has ceased when wine is clear.
10. Siphon off wine and place into wine bottles.

11. Place in wine bottles and cork; leave upright for three days and store on sides in racks for six months.

Apricot Wine Recipe

Ingredients

3 lbs. Sweet ripe apricots

1/2 gal. Water

2 lbs. Sugar

1 pkg. Yeast Nutrient

1 pkg. Wine Yeast

Directions

1. Prepare fruit by peeling, removing cores and wash fruit, chop into small pieces.
2. Boil water and cool, add sugar, stir until sugar is dissolved.
3. Add sugar water and fruit to five gallon crock. Cover for 24 hours.
4. Add yeast nutrient, wine yeast to the mixture stir with a wooden spoon. Cover and keep in a 70 degree place for three days.
5. Strain off the liquid with a cheese cloth into a gallon jug. Put an air lock on the end of the jug.
6. Place in a dry cool place 65 degrees F. for three weeks.
7. Siphon the wine off the sedimentation. Do not mix.
8. Place in clean jug and continue the process until fermentation ceases.
9. The fermentation has ceased when wine is clear.
10. Siphon off wine and place into wine bottles.
11. Place in wine bottles and cork; leave upright for three days and store on sides in racks for six months.

Apricot/Peach Wine Recipe

Ingredients

1 gal. Peaches

3 gal. Water

2 lbs. Sugar

1 pkg. Yeast Nutrient

1 pkg. Wine Yeast

Directions

1. Prepare fruit by peeling, removing cores and wash fruit, chop into small pieces.
2. Boil water and cool, add sugar, stir until sugar is dissolved.
3. Add sugar Water and fruit to five gallon crock. Cover for 24 hours.
4. Add yeast nutrient, wine yeast to the mixture stir with a wooden spoon. Cover and keep in a 70 degree place for three days.
5. Strain off the liquid with a cheese cloth into a gallon jug. Put an air lock on the end of the jug.
6. Place in a dry cool place 65 degrees F. for three weeks.
7. Siphon the wine off the sedimentation. Do not mix.
8. Place in clean jug and continue the process until fermentation ceases.
9. The fermentation has ceased when wine is clear.
10. Siphon off wine and place into wine bottles.
11. Place in wine bottles and cork; leave upright for three days and store on sides in racks for six months.

Blackberry Wine Recipe

Ingredients

2 gal. Blackberries

1 gal. Water

2 1/2 lbs. Sugar

1 pkg. Wine Yeast

1 pkg. Yeast Nutrient

Directions

1. Prepare fruit by peeling, removing cores and wash fruit, chop into small pieces.
2. Boil water and cool, add sugar, stir until sugar is dissolved.
3. Add sugar water and fruit to five gallon crock. Cover for 24 hours.
4. Add yeast nutrient, wine yeast to the mixture stir with a wooden spoon. Cover and keep in a 70 degree place for three days.
5. Strain off the liquid with a cheese cloth into a gallon jug. Put an air lock on the end of the jug.
6. Place in a dry cool place 65 degrees F. for three weeks.
7. Siphon the wine off the sedimentation. Do not mix.
8. Place in clean jug and continue the process until fermentation ceases.
9. The fermentation has ceased when wine is clear.
10. Siphon off wine and place into wine bottles.
11. Place in wine bottles and cork; leave upright for three days and store on sides in racks for six months.

Blackberry/Wild Plum Wine Recipe

Ingredients

2 gal. Blackberries

1 gal. Wild Plums, pitted

1 gal. Water

2 1/2 lbs. Sugar

1 pkg. Wine Yeast

1 pkg. Yeast Nutrient

Directions

1. Prepare fruit by peeling, removing cores and wash fruit, chop into small pieces.
2. Boil water and cool, add sugar, stir until sugar is dissolved.
3. Add sugar water and fruit to five gallon crock. Cover for 24 hours.
4. Add yeast nutrient, wine yeast to the mixture stir with a wooden spoon. Cover and keep in a 70 degree place for three days.
5. Strain off the liquid with a cheese cloth into a gallon jug. Put an air lock on the end of the jug.
6. Place in a dry cool place 65 degrees F. for three weeks.
7. Siphon the wine off the sedimentation. Do not mix.
8. Place in clean jug and continue the process until fermentation ceases.
9. The fermentation has ceased when wine is clear.
10. Siphon off wine and place into wine bottles.
11. Place in wine bottles and cork; leave upright for three days and store on sides in racks for six months.

Blueberry Wine Recipe

Ingredients

2 gal. Blueberries

1 gal. Water

2 lbs. Sugar

1 pkg. Yeast Nutrient

1 pkg. Wine Yeast

Directions

1. Prepare fruit by peeling, removing cores and wash fruit, chop into small pieces.
2. Boil water and cool, add sugar, stir until sugar is dissolved.
3. Add sugar water and fruit to five gallon crock. Cover for 24 hours.
4. Add yeast nutrient, wine yeast to the mixture stir with a wooden spoon. Cover and keep in a 70 degree place for three days.
5. Strain off the liquid with a cheese cloth into a gallon jug. Put an air lock on the end of the jug.
6. Place in a dry cool place 65 degrees F. for three weeks.
7. Siphon the wine off the sedimentation. Do not mix.
8. Place in clean jug and continue the process until fermentation ceases.
9. The fermentation has ceased when wine is clear.
10. Siphon off wine and place into wine bottles.
11. Place in wine bottles and cork; leave upright for three days and store on sides in racks for six months.

Cherry Peppermint Wine Recipe

Ingredients

1 gal. of Red Cherries

1 gal. of Water

2 lbs. Sugar

1 pkg. Yeast Nutrient

1 pkg. Wine Yeast

1/2 cup Peppermint

Directions

1. Prepare fruit by peeling, removing cores and wash fruit, chop into small pieces.
2. Boil water and cool, add sugar, stir until sugar is dissolved.
3. Add sugar water and fruit to five gallon crock. Cover for 24 hours.
4. Add yeast nutrient, wine yeast to the mixture stir with a wooden spoon. Cover and keep in a 70 degree place for three days.
5. Strain off the liquid with a cheese cloth into a gallon jug. Put an air lock on the end of the jug.
6. Place in a dry cool place 65 degrees F. for three weeks.
7. Siphon the wine off the sedimentation. Do not mix.
8. Place in clean jug and continue the process until fermentation ceases.
9. The fermentation has ceased when wine is clear.
10. Siphon off wine and place into wine bottles.
11. Place in wine bottles and cork; leave upright for three days and store on sides in racks for six months.

Crabapple Wine Recipe

Ingredients

1 gal. Crabapples

1 gal. Water

2 lbs. Sugar

1 pkg. Yeast Nutrient

1 pkg. Wine Yeast

Directions

1. Prepare fruit by peeling, removing cores and wash fruit, chop into small pieces.
2. Boil water and cool, add sugar, stir until sugar is dissolved.
3. Add sugar water and fruit to five gallon crock. Cover for 24 hours.
4. Add yeast nutrient, wine yeast to the mixture stir with a wooden spoon. Cover and keep in a 70 degree place for three days.
5. Strain off the liquid with a cheese cloth into a gallon jug. Put an air lock on the end of the jug.
6. Place in a dry cool place 65 degrees F. for three weeks.
7. Siphon the wine off the sedimentation. Do not mix.
8. Place in clean jug and continue the process until fermentation ceases.
9. The fermentation has ceased when wine is clear.
10. Siphon off wine and place into wine bottles.
11. Place in wine bottles and cork; leave upright for three days and store on sides in racks for six months.

Cranberry/Wild Grape Wine Recipe

Ingredients

1 gal. Cranberries

1 gal. wild Grapes

1 gal. Water

2 lbs. Sugar

1 pkg. Yeast Nutrient

1 pkg. Wine Yeast

Directions

1. Prepare fruit by peeling, removing cores and wash fruit, chop into small pieces.
2. Boil water and cool, add sugar, stir until sugar is dissolved.
3. Add sugar water and fruit to five gallon crock. Cover for 24 hours.
4. Add yeast nutrient, wine yeast to the mixture stir with a wooden spoon. Cover and keep in a 70 degree place for three days.
5. Strain off the liquid with a cheese cloth into a gallon jug. Pot an air lock on the end of the jug.
6. Place in a dry cool place 65 degrees F. for three weeks.
7. Siphon the wine off the sedimentation. Do not mix.
8. Place in clean jug and continue the process until fermentation ceases.
9. The fermentation has ceased when wine is clear.
10. Siphon off wine and place into wine bottles.
11. Place in wine bottles and cork; leave upright for three days and store on sides in racks for six months.

Cherry/Blackberry Wine Recipe

Ingredients

1 gal. Blackberries

1 gal. Red Cherries

1 gal. Water

2 lbs. Sugar

1 pkg. Yeast Nutrient

1 pkg. Wine Yeast

Directions

1. Prepare fruit by peeling, removing cores and wash fruit, chop into small pieces.
2. Boil water and cool, add sugar, stir until sugar is dissolved.
3. Add sugar water and fruit to five gallon crock. Cover for 24 hours.
4. Add yeast nutrient, wine yeast to the mixture stir with a wooden spoon. Cover and keep in a 70 degree place for three days.
5. Strain off the liquid with a cheese cloth into a gallon jug. Put an airlock on the end of the jug.
6. Place in a dry cool place 65 degrees F. for three weeks.
7. Siphon the wine off the sedimentation. Do not mix.
8. Place in clean jug and continue the process until fermentation ceases.
9. The fermentation has ceased when wine is clear.
10. Siphon off wine and place into wine bottles.
11. Place in wine bottles and cork; leave upright for three days and store on sides in racks for six months.

Delicious Apple Wine

2 gallons Delicious Red Apples

1 gallon water

11/2 pounds sugar

1 package yeast nutrient

I package wine yeast

Directions

1. Prepare fruit by peeling, removing core and stems. Chop into pieces
2. Boil water and cool, add sugar and stir until sugar is dissolved
3. Add sugar eater and fruit to a five gallon crock. Cover for 24 hours.
4. Add yeast nutrient, wine yeast to the mixture stir with wooden spoon. Cover and keep in a 70 degree place for three days.
5. Strain off the liquid with cheese cloth. Store in a gallon jug in a cool place.
6. Siphon the wine off the sedimentation. Do not mix.
7. Continue process until liquid becomes clear.
8. Store in wine bottles and cork; leave upright for three days and the store on sides for six months.

Note: For Green Apple Wine - Follow the Same Process

Dewberry Wine

4 gallons Dewberries, freshly picked

1 gallon water

2 pounds sugar

1 pkg yeast nutrient

1 package wine nutrient

Directions

1. Prepare dewberries by removing stems and bruised berries
2. Boil water and add sugar to the water stir until dissolved
3. Add to dewberries and place in a cleave five gallon crock. Cover for 24 hours.
4. Add yeast nutrient, wine yeast to the mixture stir with a wooden spoon.
5. Cover and keep in a 70 degree cool place for three days.
6. Strain off liquid with a cheese cloth into a gallon jug. Put an air lock on the top of the jug!
7. Place in a dry cool place 65 degree F for three weeks
8. Siphon the wine off the sedimentation. Do not mix
9. Put wine into clean jug and continue the process until fermentation ceases.
10. Siphon off wine and place into wine bottles; cork and leave in wine bottles until use. Store in cool place.

Mayhaw Wine

Ingredients

4 gal. Mayhaws

1 gal. Water

4 cups Sugar

1 pkg. Yeast Nutrient

1 pkg. Wine Yeast

Directions

1. Prepare fruit by peeling, removing cores and wash fruit, chop into small pieces.
2. Boil water and cool, add sugar, stir until sugar is dissolved.
3. Add sugar water and fruit to five gallon crock. Cover for 24 hours.
4. Add yeast nutrient, wine yeast to the mixture stir with a wooden spoon. Cover and keep in a 70 degree place for three days.
5. Strain off the liquid with a cheese cloth into a gallon jug. Put an air lock on the end of the jug.
6. Place in a dry cool place 65 degrees F. for three weeks.
7. Siphon the wine off the sedimentation. Do not mix.
8. Place in clean jug and continue the process until fermentation ceases.
9. The fermentation has ceased when wine is clear.
10. Siphon off wine and place into wine bottles.
11. Place in wine bottles and cork; leave upright for three days and store on sides in racks for six months.

Grape Blackberry Wine Recipe

Ingredients

1 gal. Tokay Grapes

1 gal. Blackberries

2 gal. Water

2 lbs. Sugar

1 pkg. Yeast Nutrient

1 pkg. Wine Yeast

Directions

1. Prepare fruit by peeling, removing cores and wash fruit, chop into small pieces.
2. Boil water and cool, add sugar, stir until sugar is dissolved.
3. Add sugar water and fruit to five gallon crock. Cover for 24 hours.
4. Add yeast nutrient, wine yeast to the mixture stir with a wooden spoon. Cover and keep in a 70 degree place for three days.
5. Strain off the liquid with a cheese cloth into a gallon jug. Put an air lock on the end of the jug.
6. Place in a dry cool place 65 degrees F. for three weeks.
7. Siphon the wine off the sedimentation. Do not mix.
8. Place in clean jug and continue the process until fermentation ceases.
9. The fermentation has ceased when wine is clear.
10. Siphon off wine and place into wine bottles.
11. Place in wine bottles and cork; leave upright for three days and store on sides in racks for six months.

Green Plum Wine

Ingredients

2 lbs. Plums (seed green plum)

1 gal. Water

2 lbs. Sugar

1 pkg. Yeast Nutrient

1 pkg. Wine Yeast

Directions

1. Prepare fruit by peeling, removing cores and wash fruit, chop into small pieces.
2. Boil water and cool, add sugar, stir until sugar is dissolved.
3. Add sugar water and fruit to five gallon crock. Cover for 24 hours.
4. Add yeast nutrient, wine yeast to the mixture stir with a wooden spoon. Cover and keep in a 70 degree place for three days.
5. Strain off the liquid with a cheese cloth into a gallon jug. Put an air lock on the end of the jug.
6. Place in a dry cool place 65 degrees F. for three weeks.
7. Siphon the wine off the sedimentation. Do not mix.
8. Place in clean jug and continue the process until fermentation ceases.
9. The fermentation has ceased when wine is clear.
10. Siphon off wine and place into wine bottles.
11. Place in wine bottles and cork; leave upright for three days and store on sides in racks for six months.

Honeydew Melon Wine

Ingredients

5 gal. Honeydew melons, chopped

1 gal. Water

1 cup Sugar

1 pkg. Yeast Nutrient

1 pkg. Wine Yeast

Directions

1. Prepare fruit by peeling, removing cores and wash fruit, chop into small pieces.
2. Boil water and cool, add sugar, stir until sugar is dissolved.
3. Add sugar water and fruit to five gallon crock. Cover for 24 hours.
4. Add yeast nutrient, wine yeast to the mixture stir with a wooden spoon. Cover and keep in a 70 degree place for three days.
5. Strain off the liquid with a cheese cloth into a gallon jug. Put an air lock on the end of the jug.
6. Place in a dry cool place 65 degrees F. for three weeks.
7. Siphon the wine off the sedimentation. Do not mix.
8. Place in clean jug and continue the process until fermentation ceases.
9. The fermentation has ceased when wine is clear.
10. Siphon off wine and place into wine bottles.
11. Place in wine bottles and cork; leave upright for three days and store on sides in racks for six months.

Musk Melon Wine Recipe

4 gal. Musk melons

2 gal. Water

2 lbs. Sugar

I pkg. Yeast Nutrient

1 pkg. Wine Yeast

Directions

1. Prepare fruit by peeling, removing cores and wash fruit, chop into small pieces.
2. Boil water and cool, add sugar, stir until sugar is dissolved.
3. Add sugar water and fruit to five gallon crock. Cover for 24 hours.
4. Add yeast nutrient, wine yeast to the mixture stir with a wooden spoon. Cover and keep in a 70 degree place for three days.
5. Strain off the liquid with a cheese cloth into a gallon jug. Put an air lock on the end of the jug.
6. Place in a dry cool place 65 degrees F. for three weeks.
7. Siphon the wine off the sedimentation. Do not mix.
8. Place in clean jug and continue the process until fermentation ceases.
9. The fermentation has ceased when wine is clear.
10. Siphon off wine and place into wine bottles.
11. Place in wine bottles and cork; leave upright for three days and store on sides in racks for six months.

Nectarine Wine Recipe

Ingredients

3 lbs. Nectarines

1 gal. Water

2 lbs. Sugar

1 pkg. Yeast Nutrient

1 pkg. Wine Yeast

Directions

1. Prepare fruit by peeling, removing cores and wash fruit, chop into small pieces.
2. Boil water and cool, add sugar, stir until sugar is dissolved.
3. Add sugar water and fruit to five gallon crock. Cover for 24 hours.
4. Add yeast nutrient, wine yeast to the mixture stir with a wooden spoon. Cover and keep in a 70 degree place for three days.
5. Strain off the liquid with a cheese cloth into a gallon jug. Put an air lock on the end of the jug.
6. Place in a dry cool place 65 degrees F. for three weeks.
7. Siphon the wine off the sedimentation. Do not mix.
8. Place in clean jug and continue the process until fermentation ceases.
9. The fermentation has ceased when wine is clear.
10. Siphon off wine and place into wine bottles.
11. Place in wine bottles and cork; leave upright for three days and store on sides in racks for six months.

Peach/Grapefruit Wine Recipe

Ingredients

1 gal. Peaches, diced

1/2 gal. Grapefruit Juice

1 gal. Water

2 lbs. Sugar

1 pkg. Yeast Nutrient

1 pkg. Wine Yeast

Directions

1. Prepare fruit by peeling, removing cores and wash fruit, chop into small pieces.
2. Boil water and cool, add sugar, stir until sugar is dissolved.
3. Add sugar water and fruit to five gallon crock. Cover for 24 hours.
4. Add yeast nutrient, wine yeast to the mixture stir with a wooden spoon. Cover and keep in a 70 degree place for three days.
5. Strain off the liquid with a cheese cloth into a gallon jug. Put an air lock on the end of the jug.
6. Place in a dry cool place 65 degrees F. for three weeks.
7. Siphon the wine off the sedimentation. Do not mix.
8. Place in clean jug and continue the process until fermentation ceases.
9. The fermentation has ceased when wine is clear.
10. Siphon off wine and place into wine bottles.
11. Place in wine bottles and cork; leave upright for three days and store on sides in racks for six months.

Pear Wine Recipe

Ingredients

1 gal. Bartlett Pears, peeled, diced

1 gal. Water

2 lbs. Sugar

1 pkg. Yeast Nutrient

1 pkg. Wine Yeast

Directions

1. Prepare fruit by peeling, removing cores and wash fruit, chop into small pieces.
2. Boil water and cool, add sugar, stir until sugar is dissolved.
3. Add sugar water and fruit to five gallon crock. Cover for 24 hours.
4. Add yeast nutrient, wine yeast to the mixture stir with a wooden spoon. Cover and keep in a 70 degree place for three days.
5. Strain off the liquid with a cheese cloth into a gallon jug. Put an air lock on the end of the jug.
6. Place in a dry cool place 65 degrees F. for three weeks.
7. Siphon the wine off the sedimentation. Do not mix.
8. Place in clean jug and continue the process until fermentation ceases.
9. The fermentation has ceased when wine is clear.
10. Siphon off wine and place into wine bottles.
11. Place in wine bottles and cork; leave upright for three days and store on sides in racks for six months.

Post Oak Grape Wine Recipe

Ingredients

1 gal. Red Oak Grape

2 gal. Water

2 lbs. Sugar

1 pkg. Yeast Nutrient

1 pkg. Wine Yeast

Directions

1. Prepare fruit by peeling, removing cores and wash fruit, chop into small pieces.
2. Boil water and cool, add sugar, stir until sugar is dissolved.
3. Add sugar water and fruit to five gallon crock. Cover for 24 hours.
4. Add yeast nutrient, wine yeast to the mixture stir with a wooden spoon. Cover and keep in a 70 degree place for three days.
5. Strain off the liquid with a cheese cloth into a gallon jug. Put an air lock on the end of the jug.
6. Place in a dry cool place 65 degrees F. for three weeks.
7. Siphon the wine off the sedimentation. Do not mix.
8. Place in clean jug and continue the process until fermentation ceases.
9. The fermentation has ceased when wine is clear.
10. Siphon off wine and place into wine bottles.
11. Place in wine bottles and cork; leave upright for three days and store on sides in racks for six months.

Raspberry/Strawberry Wine Recipe

Ingredients

1 gal. Raspberries

1 gal. Strawberries

2 gal. Water

2 1/2 lbs. Sugar

1 pkg. Yeast Nutrient

1 pkg. Wine Yeast

Directions

1. Prepare fruit by peeling, removing cores and wash fruit, chop into small pieces.
2. Boil water and cool, add sugar, stir until sugar is dissolved.
3. Add sugar water and fruit to five gallon crock. Cover for 24 hours.
4. Add yeast nutrient, wine yeast to the mixture stir with a wooden spoon. Cover and keep in a 70 degree place for three days.
5. Strain off the liquid with a cheese cloth into a gallon jug. Put an air lock on the end of the jug.
6. Place in a dry cool place 65 degrees F. for three weeks.
7. Siphon the wine off the sedimentation. Do not mix.
8. Place in clean jug and continue the process until fermentation ceases.
9. The fermentation has ceased when wine is clear.
10. Siphon off wine and place into wine bottles.
11. Place in wine bottles and cork; leave upright for three days and store on sides in racks for six months.

Strawberry/Mango Wine

1 gallon Strawberries, fresh

1/2 gallon mangoes

2 gallons water

1 pound sugar

1 package yeast nutrient

1 package wine yeast

Directions

1. Prepare fruit by removing stems from strawberries, remove cores, peel and dice mangoes.
2. Boil water and add sugar. Stir until sugar is dissolved. Cool
3. Add sugar water and fruit to a five gallon jig! Cover for 24 hours.
4. Add yeast nutrient, wine yeast to the mixture, stir with s wooden spoon. Cover and keep in a 70 degree place for three days!
1. 5, Strain off the liquid with s cheese cloth into a gallon jug. Put ins air lock on the end of a jug.
5. Place in a dry cool place 65 degrees F. for three weeks.
6. Siphon off the wine from the sedimentations. Do not mix.
7. Continue the process until fermentation has stopped.
8. Siphon off wine and then place in wine bottles.
9. Cork wine and leave upright for three days and then store on sides for six months.

NOTE: STRAWBERRY/PERSIMMON WINE- FOLLOW THE ABOVE RECIPE USE ONLY 1/2 GALLON OF RIPE PERSIMMONS PEELED AND CORED.

STRAWBERRY —PAPAYA WINE: Follow recipe use -2 gallons strawberries and 1/4 gallon of papayas.

Strawberry/Pineapple Wine Recipe

Ingredients

1 gal. Strawberries

2-46 ounce cans Pineapple Juice

1 gal. Water

2 lbs. Sugar

1 pkg. Yeast Nutrient

1 pkg. Wine Yeast

Directions

1. Prepare fruit by peeling, removing cores and wash fruit, chop into small pieces.
2. Boil water and cool, add sugar, stir until sugar is dissolved.
3. Add sugar water and fruit to five gallon crock. Cover for 24 hours.
4. Add yeast nutrient, wine yeast to the mixture stir with a wooden spoon. Cover and keep in a 70 degree place for three days.
5. Strain off the liquid with a cheese cloth into a gallon jug. Put an air lock on the end of the jug.
6. Place in a dry cool place 65 degrees F. for three weeks.
7. Siphon the wine off the sedimentation. Do not mix.
8. Place in clean jug and continue the process until fermentation ceases.
9. The fermentation has ceased when wine is clear.
10. Siphon off wine and place into wine bottles.

11. Place in wine bottles and cork; leave upright for three days and store on sides in racks for six months.

Kiwi Wine Recipe

Ingredients

5 gal. Kiwis, peeled & chopped finely

1 gal. Water

4 cups Sugar

1 pkg. Yeast Nutrient

1 pkg. Wine Yeast

Directions

1. Prepare fruit by peeling, removing cores and wash fruit, chop into small pieces.
2. Boil water and cool, add sugar, stir until sugar is dissolved.
3. Add sugar water and fruit to five gallon crock. Cover for 24 hours.
4. Add yeast nutrient, wine yeast to the mixture stir with a wooden spoon. Cover and keep in a 70 degree place for three days.
5. Strain off the liquid with a cheese cloth into a gallon jug. Put an air lock on the end of the jug.
6. Place in a dry cool place 65 degrees F. for three weeks.
7. Siphon the wine off the sedimentation. Do not mix.
8. Place in clean jug and continue the process until fermentation ceases.
9. The fermentation has ceased when wine is clear.
10. Siphon off wine and place into wine bottles.
11. Place in wine bottles and cork; leave upright for three days and store on sides in racks for six months.

Scuppernong Wine

Ingredients

5 gal. Scuppernongs

2 gal. Water

2 lbs. Sugar

1 pkg. Yeast Nutrient

1 pkg. Wine Yeast

Directions

1. Prepare fruit by peeling, removing cores and wash fruit, chop into small pieces.
2. Boil water and cool, add sugar, stir until sugar is dissolved.
3. Add sugar water and fruit to five gallon crock. Cover for 24 hours.
4. Add yeast nutrient, wine yeast to the mixture stir with a wooden spoon. Cover and keep in a 70 degree place for three days.
5. Strain off the liquid with a cheese cloth into a gallon jug. Put an air lock on the end of the jug.
6. Place in a dry cool place 65 degrees F. for three weeks.
7. Siphon the wine off the sedimentation. Do not mix.
8. Place in clean jug and continue the process until fermentation ceases.
9. The fermentation has ceased when wine is clear.
10. Siphon off wine and place into wine bottles.
11. Place in wine bottles and cork; leave upright for three days and store on sides in racks for six months.

Strawberry Wine Recipe

Ingredients

5 lbs. Fresh Ripe Strawberries

1 gal. Water

2 lbs. Sugar

1 pkg. Yeast Nutrient

1 pkg. Wine Yeast

Directions

1. Prepare fruit by peeling, removing cores and wash fruit, chop into small pieces.
2. Boil water and cool, add sugar, stir until sugar is dissolved.
3. Add sugar water and fruit to five gallon crock. Cover for 24 hours.
4. Add yeast nutrient, wine yeast to the mixture stir with a wooden spoon. Cover and keep in a 70 degree place for three days.
5. Strain off the liquid with a cheese cloth into a gallon jug. Put an air lock on the end of the jug.
6. Place in a dry cool place 65 degrees F. for three weeks.
7. Siphon the wine off the sedimentation. Do not mix.
8. Place in clean jug and continue the process until fermentation ceases.
9. The fermentation has ceased when wine is clear.
10. Siphon off wine and place into wine bottles.
11. Place in wine bottles and cork; leave upright for three days and store on sides in racks for six months.

Strawberry Mint Wine Recipe

Ingredients

1 gal. Strawberries, chopped

1 cup Mint, fresh, chopped

1 gal. Water

2 lbs. Sugar

1 pkg. Yeast Nutrient

1 pkg. Wine Yeast

Directions

1. Prepare fruit by peeling, removing cores and wash fruit, chop into small pieces.
2. Boil water and cool, add sugar, stir until sugar is dissolved.
3. Add sugar water and fruit to five gallon crock. Cover for 24 hours.
4. Add yeast nutrient, wine yeast to the mixture stir with a wooden spoon. Cover and keep in a 70 degree place for three days.
5. Strain off the liquid with a cheese cloth into a gallon jug. Put an air lock on the end of the jug.
6. Place in a dry cool place 65 degrees F. for three weeks.
7. Siphon the wine off the sedimentation. Do not mix.
8. Place in clean jug and continue the process until fermentation ceases.
9. The fermentation has ceased when wine is clear.
10. Siphon off wine and place into wine bottles.
11. Place in wine bottles and cork; leave upright for three days and store on sides in racks for six months.

Strawberry/Watermelon Wine Recipe

Ingredients

1 gal. Strawberries

1/2 gal. Watermelons

1 gal. Water

2 lbs. Sugar

1 pkg. Yeast Nutrient pkg. Wine Yeast

Directions

1. Prepare fruit by peeling, removing cores and wash fruit, chop into small pieces.
2. Boil water and cool, add sugar, stir until sugar is dissolved.
3. Add sugar water and fruit to five gallon crock. Cover for 24 hours.
4. Add yeast nutrient, wine yeast to the mixture stir with a wooden spoon. Cover and keep in a 70 degree place for three days.
5. Strain off the liquid with a cheese cloth into a gallon jug. Put an air lock on the end of the jug.
6. Place in a dry cool place 65 degrees F. for three weeks.
7. Siphon the wine off the sedimentation. Do not mix.
8. Place in clean jug and continue the process until fermentation ceases.
9. The fermentation has ceased when wine is clear.
10. Siphon off wine and place into wine bottles.
11. Place in wine bottles and cork; leave upright for three days and store on sides in racks for six months.

Sweet Potato Wine Recipe

Ingredients

10 small Sweet Potatoes

1 gal. Water

2 lbs. Sugar

1 pkg. Yeast Nutrient

1 pkg. Wine Yeast

Directions

1. Prepare fruit by peeling, removing cores and wash fruit, chop into small pieces.
2. Boil water and cool, add sugar, stir until sugar is dissolved.
3. Add sugar water and fruit to five gallon crock. Cover for 24 hours.
4. Add yeast nutrient, wine yeast to the mixture stir with a wooden spoon. Cover and keep in a 70 degree place for three days.
5. Strain off the liquid with a cheese cloth into a gallon jug. Put an air lock on the end of the jug.
6. Place in a dry cool place 65 degrees F. for three weeks.
7. Siphon the wine off the sedimentation. Do not mix.
8. Place in clean jug and continue the process until fermentation ceases.
9. The fermentation has ceased when wine is clear.
10. Siphon off wine and place into wine bottles.
11. Place in wine bottles and cork; leave upright for three days and store on sides in racks for six months.

Watermelon/Blackberry Wine Recipe

Ingredients

5 lbs. Melons, Blackberries, cut and diced

1 gal. Water

3 lbs. Sugar

1 pkg. Yeast Nutrient

1 pkg. Wine Yeast

Directions

1. Prepare fruit by peeling, removing cores and wash fruit, chop into small pieces.
2. Boil water and cool, add sugar, stir until sugar is dissolved.
3. Add sugar water and fruit to five gallon crock. Cover for 24 hours.
4. Add yeast nutrient, wine yeast to the mixture stir with a wooden spoon. Cover and keep in a 70 degree place for three days.
5. Strain off the liquid with a cheese cloth into a gallon jug. Put an air lock on the end of the jug.
6. Place in a dry cool place 65 degrees F. for three weeks.
7. Siphon the wine off the sedimentation. Do not mix.
8. Place in clean jug and continue the process until fermentation ceases.
9. The fermentation has ceased when wine is clear.
10. Siphon off wine and place into wine bottles.
11. Place in wine bottles and cork; leave upright for three days and store on sides in racks for six months.

Wild Green Plum Wine Recipe

Ingredients

2 lbs. Plums

1 gal. Water

2 lbs. Sugar

1 pkg. Yeast Nutrient

1 pkg. Wine Yeast

Directions

1. Prepare fruit by peeling, removing cores and wash fruit, chop into small pieces.
2. Boil water and cool, add sugar, stir until sugar is dissolved.
3. Add sugar water and fruit to five gallon crock. Cover for 24 hours.
4. Add yeast nutrient, wine yeast to the mixture stir with a wooden spoon. Cover and keep in a 70 degree place for three days.
5. Strain off the liquid with a cheese cloth into a gallon jug. Put an air lock on the end of the jug.
6. Place in a dry cool place 65 degrees F. for three weeks.
7. Siphon the wine off the sedimentation. Do not mix.
8. Place in clean jug and continue the process until fermentation ceases.
9. The fermentation has ceased when wine is clear.
10. Siphon off wine and place into wine bottles.
11. Place in wine bottles and cork; leave upright for three days and store on sides in racks for six months.

Wild Plum/Pear Wine Recipe

Ingredients

1 gal. wild Plums, pits removed

1 gal. Pears, diced

1 gal. Water

2 lbs. Sugar

1 pkg. Yeast Nutrient

1 pkg. Wine Yeast

Directions

1. Prepare fruit by peeling, removing cores and wash fruit, chop into small pieces.
2. Boil water and cool, add sugar, stir until sugar is dissolved.
3. Add sugar water and fruit to five gallon crock. Cover for 24 hours.
4. Add yeast nutrient, wine yeast to the mixture stir with a wooden spoon. Cover and keep in a 70 degree place for three days.
5. Strain off the liquid with a cheese cloth into a gallon jug. Put an air lock on the end of the jug.
6. Place in a dry cool place 65 degrees F. for three weeks.
7. Siphon the wine off the sedimentation. Do not mix.
8. Place in clean jug and continue the process until fermentation ceases.
9. The fermentation has ceased when wine is clear.
10. Siphon off wine and place into wine bottles.
11. Place in wine bottles and cork; leave upright for three days and store on sides in racks for six months.

INDEPENDENT SCHOOLS

Central State University

Wilberforce, Ohio

History: Founded 1887 (Public, Rural, Methodist Episcopal and African Methodist Episcopal Church (AME)

Enrollment: 2,798

Degrees Granted: Baccalaureate and Master degrees

Established – – Tarnawa Springs, Ohio — 1856

Name of Band - Invincible Marching Marauders

Sports — Football, basketball (w&m), football, cross-country, track & field (w&m), volleyball, tennis, golf

CLASSIC BOWL GAME:1) Dayton Classic Central State University vs University of Dayton, Dayton Stadium Cheyney University of Pennsylvania Cheyney, PA

History: Founded — 1837 — Oldest Institution of Higher Learning for African Americans(275 ACRES)

ENROLLMENT: 1000+

DEGREES GRANTED: BACHELORS AND MASTERS DEGREES

Colors — Blue & White

Nickname — Wolves

Stadium — O'Shields Stevenson — The Pennsylvania State Athletic Conference (PSAC)

Sports — Football, basketball (m&w), volleyball, tennis, bowling, cross-country track (rn&w), soccer (m)

CLASSIC BOWL GAMES: 1) Wade Wilson Classic —Cheyney University vs, Bowie State University @ Cheyney

Lincoln University

Pennsylvania

Name of School — Lincoln University

Named for President Abraham Lincoln

Date Established — 1854

School Colors — Blue & Orange

Nickname/Mascot — Lions

Name of Stadium

Sports — Baseball, basketball (m&w), cross-country (m&w), football, soccer (m&w), tennis (m&w), track & field (m&w), softball, bowling (w), volleyball (w)

CLASSIC BOWL CLASSIC

5th Prince George Classic

Bowie State University vs Lincoln University, Penn

LANGSTON UNIVERSITY

LANGSTON, OKLAHOMA

MOTTO: Education for Service

History: Founded in 1867 Public Land-grant, Rural

Enrollment: 3,922

DEGREE GRANTED: Baccalaureate and master degrees

Colors: Navy Blue and Orange

Nickname/Mascot: Lions

NAME OF MARCHING BAND: Langston University Marching Pride Band **Name of Stadium:** Lions Stadium

Sports: Basketball, football **CLASSIC BOWL GAME: 1) McGee Classic - Tulsa**

Lincoln University

Lincoln, Missouri

Name of School — Lincoln University of Missouri

Established — 1866 (Land Grant)

Colors - Navy Blue & White

Mascot — Blue Tiger

Conference — Heartland Conference

School founded by the 62nd and 65th Colored Infantries

TENNESSEE STATE UNIVERSITY

NASHVILLE, TENN

MOTTO: Think, Work, Serve

Histor **Public, Land-grant, 500 acres**

ENROLLMENT: 10,000

DEGREES GRANTED: BACCALAUREATES AND MASTERS DEGREES

School Colors: BLUE AND WHITE

Nickname: Tigers

Name of Band: Tennessee State Aristocrat of Bands

Name of Stadium:

Sports: Baseball, basketball (m&w), football, indoor track, outdoor track and field, softball, tennis, volleyball, golf

Football Classics

TEXAS COLLEGE

TYLER, TEXAS

HISTORY: Founded 1894 (Christian Methodist Episcopal Church)

Enrollment: 1000+

Degrees Granted: bachelor's degree programs in art, biology, business administration, computer science, English, education, history, mathematics, music, physical education, political science, liberal studies, social work and sociology.

Nickname/Mascots: Steers/Lady Steers

SPORTS: BASEBALL, VOLLEYBALL, SOFTBALL, TRACK, BASKETBALL,

EDWARD WATERS COLLEGE

JACKSONVILLE, FLORIDA

HISTORY: FOUNDED 1866 (Private, 23 acres, Urban, African Methodist Episcopal Church)

DEGREES GRANTED: BACHELOR'S DEGREES

ENROLLMENT: 800 Students

School Colors: Purple, Orange and White

Nickname/Mascot: Tigers and Lady Tigers

Name of Stadium:

NAME OF MARCHING BAND: Edward Waters College Marching Band

Sports: Football, Baseball

CLASSIC BOWL GAMES: SOUTHERN ALABAM HERTIAGE CLASSIC

Concordia College vs. Edward Waters College —Dothan, Alabama

WEST VIRGINIA STATE UNIVERSITY

INSTITUTE, WEST VIRGINIA

Motto: A living Laboratory of Human Relations

History: Founded 1891 (Public, Suburban)

ENROLLMENT: 5,000

DEGREES GRANTED: BACHERLOR'S AND MASTER'S DEGREES SCHOOL COLORS: BLACK AND GOLD

NICKNAME: "State" or "West Virginia State"

NAME OF MARCHING BAND: The Yellow Jackets Marching Band

Mascot: Yellow Jackets

Sports: football

APPENDIX A
APPROPRIATE SIZES OF SERVINGS

MEATS
Beef- Without a bone -3 ounces of cooked meat
      -With a bone - 4 ounces
Pork — Chops -1 large or 2 small
Bacon 2 slices
Steak -4 ounces
Fish — 3 - 4 ounce servings
Poultry — Chicken —White —Wing and Breast or 2 Wings
Dark - Short thigh and Drumstick
Turkey —3 ounce Slices

VEGETABLES
Leafy greens — raw 1 cup
Leafy greens — cooked 1/2 cup

DESSERTS
Puddings — 1/2 cup
Cake — 1 Slice
Pies- 1 slice
Tarts—1 tart
Watermelon-1 Slice

BEVERAGES
Homecoming spirits — 1- 2ounce glass
Water — 8 ounce glass
Iced Beverages- 12 glass

BLACK INVENTORS AND THEIR INVENTIONS

Invention	Inventor	Invention	Inventor
PAPER	AFRICANS	SANI-PHONE	JERRY JOHNSON
CHESS	AFRICANS	WRENCH	JOHN A. JOHNSON
ALPHABET	AFRICANS	SUPER SOAKER	LONNIE JOHNSON
MEDICINE	AFRICANS	EYE PROTECTOR	P. JOHNSON
CIVILIZATION	AFRICANS	EGG BEATER	W. JOHNSON
AEROPLANE PROPELLING	JAMES S. ADAMS	DEFROSTER	FREDERICK M. JONES
BISCUIT CUTTER	A.P. ASHBOURNE	AIR CONDITIONING UNIT	FREDERICK M. JONES
FOLDING BED	L.C. BAILEY	TWO-CYCLE GAS ENGINE	FREDERICK M. JONES
COIN CHANGER	JAMES A. BAUER	INTERNAL COMBUSTION ENGINE	FREDERICK M. JONES
ROTARY ENGINE	ANDREW J. BEARD	STARTER GENERATOR	FREDERICK M. JONES
CAR COUPLER	ANDREW J. BEARD	REFRIGERATION CONTROLS	FREDERICK M. JONES
LETTER BOX	O.E. BECKET	BOTTLE CAPS	JONES & LONG
STAINLESS STEEL PADS	ALFRED BENJAMIN	CLOTHES DRESSER	JOHN H. JORDAN
CORN PLANTER	HENRY BLAIR	ELECTRIC LAMP	LATIMER & NICHOLS
COTTON PLANTER	HENRY BLAIR	PRINTING PRESS	W.A. LAVALETTE
IRONING BOARD	SARAH BOONE	LASER FUELS	LESTER LEE
PACE MAKER CONTROLS	OTIS BOYKIN	PRESSURE COOKER	MAURICE W. LEE
GUIDED-MISSILE	OTIS BOYKIN	ENVELOPE SEAL	F.W. LESLIE
TORPEDO DISCHARGER	H. BRADBERRY	WINDOW CLEANER	A.L. LEWIS
STREET SWEEPER	CHARLES BROOKS	PENCIL SHARPENER	JOHN L. LOVE
DISPOSABLE SYRINGE	PHIL BROOKS	FIRE EXTINGUISHER	TOM J. MARSHAL
HORSE BRIDLE BIT	L.F. BROWN	LOCK	W.A. MARTIN
HOME SECURITY SYSTEM	MARIE BROWN	SHOE LASTING MACHINE	JAN MATZELIGER
HORSESHOE	OSCAR E. BROWN	LUBRICATORS	ELIJAH MCCOY
LAWN MOWER	JOHN A. BURR	ROCKET CATAPULT	HUGH MACDONALD
TYPEWRITER	BURROUGH & MARSHMAN	ELEVATOR	ALEXANDER MILES
TRAIN ALARM	W.A. NUYUM	GAS MASK	GARRETT MORGAN
IMAGE CONVERTER	GEO. CARRUTHERS	TRAFFIC SIGNAL	GARRETT MORGAN
FOR RADIATION DETECTOR	GEO. CARRUTHERS	HAIR BRUSH	LYDA NEWMAN
PEANUT BUTTER	GEO. W. CARVER	HEATING FURNACE	ALICE H. PARKER
PAINTS AND STAINS	GEO. W. CARVER	AIR SHIP (BLIMP)	J.F. PICKERING
LOTIONS AND SOAPS	GEO. W. CARVER	FOLDING CHAIR	PURDY / SADGWAR
PILLOW UTILIZING AIR/WATER	LARRY E. CHRYSTIE	HAND STAMP	W.R. PURVIS
TRACK ATHLETE TRAINER	JOHN CLARK	FOUNTAIN PEN	W.W. PURVIS
AUTOMATIC FISHING REEL	GEORGE COOK	DUST PAN	L.P. RAY
ICE CREAM MOLD	A.L. CRALLE	INSECT DESTROYER GUN	A.C. RICHARDSON
HORSE RIDING SADDLE	WM. D. DAVIS	BABY BUGGY	W.H. RICHARDSON
SHOE	W.A. DEITZ	SUGAR REFINEMENT	N. RILLIEUX
PLAYER PIANO	JOSEPH DICKINSON	PRESSING COMB	WALTER SAMMONS
ARM FOR RECORD PLAYER	JOSEPH DICKINSON	HAIR DRESSING DEVICE	WALTER SAMMONS
DOOR STOP	O. DORSEY	CLOTHES DRIER	G.T. SAMPSON
DOOR KNOB	O. DORSEY	CELLULAR PHONE	HENRY SAMPSON
PHOTO PRINT WASH	CLATONIA J. DORTICUS	URINALYSIS MACHINE	DEWEY SANDERSON
PHOTO EMBOSSING MACHINE	CLATONIA J. DORTICUS	HYDRAULIC SHOCK ABSORBER	RALPH SANDERSON
POSTAL LETTER BOX	P.B. DOWNING	CURTAIN ROD	S.R. SCOTTRON
BLOOD PLASMA	DR. CHARLES DREW	MULTI-STAGE ROCKET	ADOLPH SHAMMS
TOILET (COMMODE)	T. ELKINS	LAWN SPRINKLER	J.W. SMITH
FURNITURE CASTER	DAVID A. FISHER	AUTOMATIC GEAR SHIFT	R.B. SPIKES
GUITAR	ROBERT FLEMMING JR.	REFRIGERATOR	J. STANDARD
IKENGA—GYROPLANE	DAVID GITTENS	MOP	T.W. STEWART
IKENGA/MKS—AUTOMOBILE	DAVID GITTENS	CATTLE ROPING APPARATUS	DARRYL THOMAS
SKOOTERBOARD	DAVID GITTENS	STAIRCLIMBING WHEELCHAIR	RUFUS J. WEAVER
GOLF TEE	GEORGE F. GRANT	POLYM. WATER REDUC. PAINT	MORRIS B. WILLIAMS
MOTOR	J. GREGORY	HELICOPTER	PAUL E. WILLIAMS
LANTERN	MICHAEL HARNEY	FIRE ESCAPE LADDER	J.B. WINTERS
THERMO HAIR CURLERS	SOLOMON HARPER	TELEPHONE TRANSMITTER	GRANVILLE T. WOODS
SPACE SHUTTLE RETRIEVAL ARM	WM. HARWELL	ELECTRIC CUT OFF SWITCH	GRANVILLE T. WOODS
ICE CREAM	AUGUSTUS JACKSON	RELAY INSTRUMENT	GRANVILLE T. WOODS
GAS BURNER	B.F. JACKSON	TELEPHONE SYSTEM	GRANVILLE T. WOODS
KITCHEN TABLE	H.A. JACKSON	ELECTRO MECH BRAKE	GRANVILLE T. WOODS
PROGRAM BLE REMOTE CONTROL	JOSEPH N. JACKSON	GALVANIC BATTERY	GRANVILLE T. WOODS
VIDEO COMMANDER	JOSEPH N. JACKSON	ELECTRIC RAILWAY SYSTEM	GRANVILLE T. WOODS
O.F. CABLE W/NON-MET. SHEATH	ARTIS JENKINS	ROLLER COASTER	GRANVILLE T. WOODS
BICYCLE FRAME	ISSAC R. JOHNSON	AUTO AIR BRAKE	GRANVILLE T. WOODS

 THE BLACK INVENTIONS MUSEUM

A NON-PROFIT CORPORATION • (310) 858-4602 • P.O. BOX 76122, L.A., CA. 90076

SLAVE VIGNETTES

FORMER SLAVE SAYINGS

FREEDOM

"When freedom came they called all the white people to the house first, and told them the darkies were free. Then on a day they called all the colored people down to the parade ground. They had a big stand" explained Eugene Wesley Smith, whose was a slave in Augusta." All the Yankees and some oil our leading colored man got up there and spoke, and told the negroes" You free. Don't steal! Now work and make a living. Do honest work, an honest living and support yourself and children. There are no more masters. You are free!"

"When the colored troops came in, they came in playthings

"Don't you see the lightning?
Don't you hear the thunder?
It isn't the lightning
It isn't the thunder
But the buttons on the Negro uniforms."

"The negroes shouted and carried on when they heard they were free."

Ex-Slave
Eugene Wesley Smith

FREEDOM

"The Yankee captain, Captain Grown, gathered all us negroes in the Fair ground, July or August after freedom, and he made a speech. Laswsy! I can see that crowd yet, a yelling and a —stomping! And the captain waving his arms and shouting! "We have achieved the victory over the South. Today you are all free men and free women!" "We had everybody shouting and jumping and my father and mother shouting along with the others. Everybody was happy.
Ex-Slave Edward Glenn

REFERENCES

Wikipedia, the free encyclopedia
Georgia Ex-slave narratives WPA Workers